EXTRAORDINARY PRAISE FOR

CLEAN UP YOUR ACT!

"This book is loaded with great ideas that can be put to use immediately to reduce paperwork and stress, save time, and increase efficiency and productivity."
— Stephanie A. Culp, author of *How to Get Organized When You Don't Have the Time* and *How to Conquer Clutter*

∎

"Outstanding... an absolute must for any executive who feels overwhelmed.... I feel strongly that by following many of the steps in this book, I will be able to increase my own productivity by 25% or more."
— Gloria Parker, Business Unit Executive, Health/Higher Education, IBM Corporation

∎

"Full of innovative ideas that end up in practical solutions.... It should prove to be a very powerful tool for most people who struggle with large volumes of paperwork."
— Ralph O. Doughty, Brigadier General, United States Army Reserve

∎

"Very informative... should be on the required reading list for all new executives in training."
— Darrell W. Vinson, Superintendent of Production, General Motors Corporation, CPC Group, Arlington Plant

∎

more...

"Dianna Booher's approach to the causes of paper clutter is a useful addition to the growing library of books on the topic and a relevant resource for support staff through senior management."
—Paulette Ensign, President, Organizing Solutions, Inc., founder of the New York chapter of the National Association of Professional Organizers

■

"Contains many tried and proven methods for eliminating paperwork. I am certain anyone can pick up something that would be useful in their work and/or at home."
—Francis E. Brown, Ph.D., Senior Vice President, Pennzoil Products Company, Technology Division

■

"Well written and offers a multitude of time-saving hints on organizing and reducing paperwork—at home, as well as the office."
—David E. LaBelle, Vice President, Human Resources, Island Creek Corporation

■

"Dianna Booher's 101 ideas to get paperwork organized and out of your life can improve anyone's productivity."
—Mel Strine, Exxon Co., U.S.A., Marketing Training Manager

■

"*Clean Up Your Act!* offers practical and useful solutions for reducing endless streams of paper. I highly recommend it."
—Lisa Kanarek, consultant, Everything's Organized, Dallas

■ ■ ■

DIANNA BOOHER is a business communications consultant whose Dallas-based firm specializes in corporate communication. The author of 25 books, her work has been featured in *USA Today, Working Woman, New Woman,* the *Los Angeles Times, Glamour* and many other publications.

CLEAN UP YOUR ACT!

Effective Ways to Organize Paperwork — and Get It Out of Your Life

Dianna Booher

WARNER BOOKS

A Time Warner Company

Copyright © 1992 by Dianna Booher
All rights reserved.

Warner Books, Inc., 1271 Avenue of the Americas, New York, NY 10020

W A Time Warner Company

Printed in the United States of America
First printing: October 1992
10 9 8 7 6 5 4 3 2 1

Library of Congress Cataloging-in-Publication Data
Booher, Dianna Daniels.
    Clean up your act! : effective ways to organize paperwork and get it out of your life / Dianna Booher.
        p.   cm.
    ISBN 0-446-39357-6
    1. Paperwork (Office practice)—Management.   2. Business records—Management.   I. Title.
HF5547.15.B658   1992
651.5—dc20   92-4240
                                                          CIP

Cover design by Diane Luger
Book design: H. Roberts

ACKNOWLEDGMENTS

Thank you to all those around our office who keep the paper from piling up: Belinda Blessen, Catherine Block, Polly Haase, Janet Houston-Spore, Vernon Rae, Elaine Smith, Amy Stout, Dianne Thomason, Helen Wells, and Gary Whitis.

And special thanks to Janet and Polly for help in preparing the manuscript.

As always, my love to Jeff and Lisa.

CONTENTS

INTRODUCTION

Do any of these excuses sound familiar? "My desk just *looks* cluttered—actually, I know where everything is." Or, "There's a method to this madness." Or, "I'm a busy person; I don't have time to deal with paperwork."

These are the excuses given by those covered in clutter, but here's what most bosses, subordinates, colleagues, customers, spouses, or friends think when they see the mess:

- He/she is obviously disorganized and incompetent.
- He/she can't determine priorities; therefore, I'd better not trust this person to meet a deadline.
- He/she isn't focused; no wonder we get such directives and policy statements.
- He/she is trying to look important with all this paperwork; I bet most of it is "grunt work"

that somebody else should be doing. The desks of senior executives don't look like this. Who's he/she trying to kid?
- He/she can't handle the job; otherwise, why would there be such a paperwork pileup and bottleneck?
- He/she obviously doesn't know how to delegate.
- He/she can't trust others. Why would they all have to prepare so many reports to keep him/her informed?
- It's a cinch he/she doesn't pay bills on time.
- I wonder if his/her whole life is this out-of-control.
- I don't want to route anything to him/her. That'll only mean a delay.

We spend a lot of time moving paper from one stack to another. We read something, try to decide what action to take, decide we don't want to decide, and then move it to a new pile—only to look through the pile and repeat the process the next day. For some people, the problem isn't that they handle so many pieces of paper; it's that they handle the *same* paper repeatedly.

For example, let's say you get a letter inviting you to attend a convention, seminar, or family reunion. You read the letter once, note the date, then check your calendar and see no conflict. But you can't decide whether the convention or family reunion is a good idea. The next day, you read the letter again, spend a little longer looking over the seminar agenda and studying your calendar—as if something had mysteriously changed since yesterday. Finally, you lay the letter aside and go to the next pile of easier decisions—until you gradually work your way back to the first pile again and that same convention invitation. "Now, what was this all about again?" you ask yourself. The dates? Who is speaking? You reread to refresh your memory about what it was you haven't decided on yet. Then you lay the paper aside again—only to repeat the process until the convention date passes or your calendar is filled.

A stroll through your workplace or your home can give you a clear idea of how much time this clutter habit is costing you. Do you have discount coupons for products tossed in a kitchen drawer? How much time does it take to shuffle through them to find what you need before going to the store? How many times do you decide not to bother to look because you're in a hurry? So how much time have you wasted in clipping the coupon in the first place and tossing it in the drawer?

Do you have utility bill receipts tossed in a box in the top of a closet? If you get a "past due" notice from the electric company for a bill payment you think you've paid, how much time does it take you to sort through the pile to verify that you did in fact pay the bill in question? Do you always find the receipt? How much time do you lose in sorting through the pile to discover that possibly this was the month you failed to toss the receipt in the box?

You read a good article about trade-show exhibits and toss it by your nightstand so you can clip it "when you have time." Three weeks later a colleague brings up plans for exhibiting at an upcoming trade show and you want to retrieve the article to persuade her to change the booth setup. How much time do you spend looking through the ten-inch stack of magazines and journals tossed by your nightstand?

Do you find the claim receipt for your dry cleaning in the bathroom? Do you find the agenda for your meeting on the dashboard of the car? Is the warranty to the dishwasher in the coupon drawer? Is the notice about renewing your club membership on the top of the TV?

If you've answered yes to any of these questions, clutter is gaining on you fast.

Clutter also accumulates inside desk drawers and in files marked "pending." Unrelated loose papers inside drawers or general files such as this have a way of never surfacing—at least not in time for the appropriate action. Recognize these "catch-all" places as just another form of clutter, a delayed decision about what to do with the paper or how, when, or if to take the appropriate action.

You've heard it said that a cluttered desk is the result of a cluttered mind. Let me add a twist: A cluttered desk means cluttered time.

Get in the habit of handling each piece of paper only once. If something's not worth putting in the correct, designated place the first time, it's not worth saving at all. Toss away the clutter so you can find the essential when you need it.

To get a permanent handle on your paperwork, you have to change your way of thinking about paperwork.

- Paper is not the only way, and not even the best way, to transmit or receive information.
- Paper doesn't mean power.
- Paper clogs up communication channels.
- Paperwork costs time and money to write, read, process, maintain, retrieve, and store.
- Paperwork reduces real productivity, unless your your job is pushing paper for the sake of pushing paper.
- Paperwork masks a fear to make decisions and take action.

Before you handle the paperwork in front of you, ask yourself the following questions: Do I really need to do this? Does anybody really care if I do this? Is there a quicker way to do this? Is it too late to do this? Has somebody else already done this for me? Would the job get done without this piece of paper? Could I hire someone else to do this for me? Do I need to read this? Why? Can someone else read it and act on it for me? Is the information already out-of-date? Do I want to pay to store this? Is there a duplicate somewhere?

Pay attention to the answers to these questions. If you can't avoid the paperwork in front of you at this moment, can you begin steps to eliminate the request or need for it in the future?

Think paperless action.

1. Don't Respond Too Quickly— the Instructions and Opportunities May Change

Granted, the majority of people seem to be procrastinators, waiting for that final deadline to push projects to completion. But there are those who have the opposite problem. Deadlines create anxiety and depression for them. So they always want to get a head start. As soon as they learn of a pending project or opportunity, they're off and running.

You may recognize yourself here: In college, these people were the ones who already had all the books checked out of the library when you wandered over to put together a bibliography for your term paper. They were the ones who'd already purchased the used textbooks and left to the latecomers the new, expensive texts without the answers.

In the business setting, they are the ones who've already suggested the meeting agenda and claimed credit for all the good ideas. They've already interviewed and received the job before most people know of the opening.

On the surface, these people have the right idea. They're first with the most. But consider the downside to this do-it-now compulsion.

You'll often rush to check out all the library books on the subject, only to hear others complain about the "limited availability" of resources and to hear the professor reduce the required sources from ten to two—after you've done the research.

You rush to buy the currently "hot" toy your child wants for Christmas before it's out of stock—only to find three weeks later that the item is still readily available and selling at a discount.

You prepare a complete custom proposal for a prospective client, who later phones to say that his boss "just wants the numbers" before he goes into a meeting in ten minutes. They make the buying decision without seeing the proposal, which took twelve hours to write.

My advice is *not* to despair about "jumping the gun" and then backslide into a state of procrastination, but to find the optimum state of readiness: Make sure the boss's instructions, the client's wishes, or your spouse's birthday plans are firm before you go to work on a project. Probe with questions. Verify that you understand. Test the commitment and completed actions (not promises) of the others involved *before* you strike out toward a deadline.

You'll have enough real paperwork without doing what, in the end, may become unnecessary.

2. Read Faster and with Purpose

Let's face it: When the mail advertising comes in, we can go through it in thirty seconds, dumping most. Or we can spend half an hour reading every word. But we shouldn't let those who mail to us impose on our time any more than we let those who phone us waste our time.

Now, before all of you who use direct mail in your marketing efforts tune out, let me elaborate. I didn't say to ignore your mail. Just be choosy. What many consider "junk" mail may be valuable to you personally. From your daily mail, you may glean new product or service ideas, marketing ideas, interesting statistics, solutions to your problems, or amusing anecdotes. One person's junk mail is another's treasure. But do be selective.

For those things you really want to read—and I subscribe to nineteen such publications—schedule uninterrupted reading time and get your money's worth. But for the so-so publications, the mail, the memos, and the reports that need responses from you, have an assistant preread and call your attention to things that need action. In fact, even in reading professional journals, an assistant can highlight key ideas that will be of particular interest.

Reading everything put before you should not be a compulsive habit. Read only what you really want and need to read.

3. Read Only "Close to the Event" to Avoid Rereading

For years time-management experts have told us to handle each piece of paper only once. According to these "sages," when you open the mail or receive a report on your desk, you should make an immediate decision so that you don't have to deal with that issue again.

The principle here is good: Avoid postponed decision making. But "handling" the paper once doesn't mean you must *read* it. Your "handling" of the paper may mean only noting where to file it or forwarding it to an assistant or colleague for action.

For example, if you're planning to attend a convention, there's no need to study the map of the area and review the housing choices and forms if you plan to stay in the same hotel with your clients.

If four weeks before a committee meeting you receive a company policy statement about coordinating contributions to charities, then why read that policy statement immediately? Will you forget key ideas and need to reread the statement before attending that meeting?

If you plan to attend a seminar that requires preparation of a preclass assignment, why read the instructions for writing your case study before you're ready to do the work?

In such situations, you create a duplication of effort for yourself by reading in advance and then rereading closer to your need-to-know date. Instead of a full reading when you receive such "reference" items, simply skim the headings to determine the scope of what's before you, make a mental note of the time required to read or take the later action, and then make a calendar or file note to come back to the paperwork at the appropriate time.

In these situations, do the reading only once—close to the event.

4. Keep Only One Address Book for Business and Personal Use

Don't you occasionally find yourself making personal calls during work hours and business calls from home? Why carry two address books, or worse yet, keep those two address books at different locations—home and office?

On first thought, you may consider the people you know as easy to categorize—family, community acquaintances, and friends as opposed to clients, business colleagues, or suppliers. But there are always those who fall between the cracks: Is John Graves, who is both a personal friend and president of your professional organization, listed in your personal or in your business address book?

Yes, you can categorize some names easily enough. However, the issue is not the category; it's *when* and *from where* you need to contact these people. You call your neighbor from work to check on whether the air-conditioning repairman has arrived. You call your college-age son about his overdrawn checking account when you have a break in your seminar schedule.

Why search through two card files or two address books to find the phone numbers and addresses you need? An additional benefit of merging the two references is that updating will be easier and quicker.

5. Make Business Cards Usable and Memorable

Do you find yourself shuffling through your business or regular card files repeatedly looking for that name—the one that you don't remember but that you hope will strike a familiar chord when you see it?

To make business cards that you collect useful, always make a note on them when you receive them (or at least when you get back to the office) to jog your memory. The place you met the person. The date. The reason you may want to make contact again. Then file the cards either by event, by company, or by name—whichever way you'll more likely remember the individual.

For example, will you remember the person's company name, or that she's a freelance graphic artist, or that you want to solicit her bid for preparing the Wentworth graphics? File accordingly under "Wentworth Project," or "Reston Graphic Artists," or "Graphic Artists."

And by no means should you feel obligated to keep a business card just because somebody mailed or handed it to you. Too many useless, meaningless cards simply make the ones you need difficult to find.

6. Keep Only One Calendar for Business and Personal Use

If you could truly compartmentalize your life into business, social, and home concerns, errands, responsibilities, and activities, you could patent the system and revolutionize the world order—not to mention, improve the mental health of working mothers and fathers everywhere.

In the thinking stages of keeping calendars, the two-calendar idea sounds fine. You start planning by thinking of home responsibilities, for example. On your social calendar, maybe the one you keep by the kitchen phone, you have noted the PTA meeting, Susan's recital, and your tennis date. Then when you get to work on Monday morning to plan the work week, you note on that desk calendar the meeting with client Jones, the trade-show expo you want to attend on Thursday, and the deadline for the HRD report.

But what happens when a colleague calls to say the trade-show expo hours have been extended into the evening and suggests that you wait until after work to attend together? Your business calendar looks open—but what about the social calendar?

You have to check two sources. More paperwork shuffling and time to make one decision.

Worse yet is telling your colleague the change of plans is fine—only to discover the conflict later, forcing you to make another phone call to retract your earlier decision.

The two-calendar system also adds a "merge errand list" step.

For example, at 5:00 you're ready to leave work. Your business calendar says that you need to attend a meeting of your professional organization—cocktails at 6:30, dinner at 7:30. Your business calendar also reminds you to call a client on the West Coast at 7:00, your time. So much for work commitments. Are you ready to leave the office? No, you'll need to check out your personal, home responsibilities also. So you pull out the second calendar to see that Susan wanted you to stop by the store to buy gym socks. And you need to phone Aunt Mary to wish her a happy birthday. You also need to phone home to see if your spouse has had any word about the latest rumor on department transfers.

So what do you do? Not having two bodies and

two minds to remember and carry out these activities, you "merge" your calendar notes on a single to-do list in the appropriate order:

- socks at Wal-Mart
- phone home about transfer
- cocktail party 6:30 to 7:00
- leave to call West Coast client and Aunt Mary
- attend dinner at 7:30

Why go through this extra paperwork step of merging business and personal matters? Keep only one calendar. Not only will you save time, you'll minimize schedule conflicts.

Another negative side effect of keeping two calendars is accidentally leaving off items when you transfer notes from one calendar to another, or forgetting to add items to both calendars. The more calendars you keep, the greater the chance of omissions, errors, or conflicts.

7. Clip Invitations to Your Calendar

Invitations pose a special problem: You need to decide on attendance now, but you don't need the details until later. But a decision is not always immediately possible if other pending commitments, or other people—like family—must figure into your decision to attend. What to do?

Put the invitation in your "To Do" box until you make a decision. Then take action by telephoning or writing your acceptance or regrets.

If you intend to accept the invitation, clip the announcement details to the calendar or jot them right on the calendar so you don't have to take a second step in scrambling to find the invitation when the day of the event rolls around. You'll have the time, the place, the dress, the agenda, and any other options at your fingertips.

All you'll need to do is go.

8. Use Approval Lines

The approval line is the answer to the edit-rewrite-edit-rewrite syndrome that has sapped the productivity of almost every corporation. Here's what I mean by an approval line:

To: Big Boss
From: Worker Bee
Subject: Recommendation for Distribution of Widgets
Our distribution system for widgets is working as designed...
We worker bees suggest that...
We would like to see this new system put into operation...

John K. Worker Bee
Systems Engineer

Approved by:

_____ _____
Terry A. Boss, Project Manager   Date

_____ _____
Gene P. Bigger Boss, Vice President   Date

Approval lines have several benefits:

First, they reduce a manager's urge to edit just for the sake of editing. When managers have subordinates write "for their signature," they rarely know what they want to see when they delegate the writing task. They only know what they *don't* want to see when they get the report, letter, or memo in hand. Then they retrieve a pen or pencil and go to work revising, and revising, and revising. Next they have their own secretary retype the document or send it back to the author for a rewrite. Both approaches are a waste of time unless the editing is for a good reason.

Much editing takes place as a matter of style or personal preference: "issue" changed to "matter," "I would like" changed to "I'd like," or "If we should decide to..." changed to "It appears that we may decide to..." When such style changes are the basis of the editing, then the use of the approval line tempts the boss to affix his or her signature at the bottom and "be done with it." Granted, the sentences may not be stated exactly as the boss would word them, but then the boss's name is not on the document as author but rather as "approver" of the information, action, or recommendation.

Thus, both writer and manager save time and paperwork.

Another benefit to using an approval line is a faster response time. When you send a memo or letter with no approval line, someone has to generate another piece of paper to respond or approve. And that takes time—until the boss is back in the office... until the secretary returns from vacation...until the big proposal is "out of the way." On the other hand, when the boss has only to affix his or her signature at the bottom of your original document and return it or forward it somewhere up the line, the response or action becomes faster and easier for all concerned.

Ownership is a third benefit of the approval line. When you write a document presenting a good idea, you get credit for your work because your signature is at the bottom as author. You're not simply an anonymous somebody doing the grunt work while others sign their names as if the idea originated with them.

In short, approval lines

- minimize the edit-rewrite-edit-rewrite syndrome
- prevent others from having to generate a new document to answer yours
- get a fast response
- provide pride in and document ownership of your work.

Use them whenever possible.

9. Use Response Cards and Lines

Response cards and lines work on the same principle as approval lines. Your piece of paper sent to others often requires them to generate a piece of paper in return, a process that often delays action on their part and yours.

If you want a quick, decisive response, make it easy for the person on the other end to answer. Take your cue from direct-mail advertisers. What do you think their response rate would be in selling magazine subscriptions or T-shirts if buyers had to sit down and write a formal letter to order? These direct-mail marketers have learned that the response rate increases with the ease of reply.

Follow their example. Type the response you want, along with a space for a check mark and/or signature, on a separate mail-back card or at the bottom of an in-house memo.

Here are examples:

- A memo goes out to ask employees to enroll in an upcoming project-management course. Enclosed is an enrollment form with everything completed except name, address, phone

number, and signature to be added by
the enrollee.
- An invitation from your neighborhood civic
  club asks homeowners their preferences about
  the structure of fees to support the
  homeowners association. At the bottom of the
  memo:

_____ Yes, I would like to increase our annual
dues 10% to pay for additional fitness-
center equipment.
_____ No, I would not favor an increase of 10%
in annual dues to pay for additional fitness-
center equipment.
Other things I suggest our association buy include:

Response lines and cards improve response time
and overall participation. As well as reducing the
respondents' paperwork, they also minimize the time
required to read and compile "open-ended" responses
and to take related phone calls.

Always look for ways you can help others respond quickly and easily.

10. Be Informal in Your Responses

Every memo or letter you receive does not deserve a formal response. To pick up the phone may be quicker than to write. Or you may be able simply to add your comments in a margin note or on a buck slip and pass the document on, saving everyone involved extra reading time.

Ask yourself who it is that imposes upon you the extra time required by formality. The following conversation among three executives was overheard in an elevator:

"Our real estate numbers certainly were down this month," the first executive said to his lower-ranking companion. "What happened?"

"Well, nothing to worry about if I recall. The explanations that I received seemed quite reasonable."

"Good. Could you give me a brief explanation this afternoon? Just a quick handwritten note is fine."

"Sure thing," the subordinate answered.

The elevator door opened and the senior executive who'd requested the explanation stepped off. When the elevator door closed, the middle manager spoke up to his subordinate. "Don't you dare send him a handwritten note. If you can't get it through the typing pool, bring it up and I'll have Sherrie type it."

The subordinate shrugged and agreed. What could have been a sixty-second job ultimately took an hour and a half to complete.

Our experience shows that most senior execuives aren't nearly as impressed by formality as by accuracy, speed, and thoroughness.

Prefer a fast answer to a more formal, time-consuming one.

11. Highlight/Personalize Brochures for Customers; Avoid the Form-Cover-Letter Response to Inquiries

Salespeople often overlook a simple way to customize their messages to individual customers and prospects: a marked-up brochure.

When a prospect calls with questions about your services, don't simply "drop a brochure in the mail." Customize it. Dog-ear page twelve and make a margin note: "John, here are the specs for the machine you're considering." Add gummed flags to mark certain pages or sections.

Have you "messed up" a nice brochure? On the contrary. In the customer's mind, you've taken the time to listen to her specific questions and offer specific answers. You've also saved the customer or prospect time in locating the answer herself.

You may or may not need to add a cover letter to accompany the brochure. If you do add one, make sure the message addresses the specific needs of the customer. This personal touch makes your sales literature and response stand out from the rest.

12. Stay in Touch with Friends, Colleagues, and Clients in Ways Other than Formal Business Letters

Do you write letters simply to stay in touch and build goodwill among former colleagues, friends, and clients? Do these communications often say nothing more than, "This is what I've been up to lately; how about you?" If so, your letters express the desire to stay current about the recipient's personal life or career. The only trouble is that a formal letter takes time and costs money.

On our 1991 client surveys, the average employee reports that she spends sixty-five minutes composing a one-page letter/memo. For a $40,000 employee, that translates into a cost of $20.19 per letter/memo.

Instead of formal communication, try something useful—and quicker. When you read an article that would be of interest to the colleague or client, clip it, add your business card, and send it along.

Here are a few other ideas for keeping in touch in an informal way:

• Clip newspaper stories about the client's or colleague's company and send them along with a handwritten note on your card that says simply: "Read about your Omaha division today. Sounds promising."

• Keep a supply of commercial greeting cards on hand to slip in the mail to those whose birthdays and anniversaries you've noted on your calendar. Also, consider "Thinking of You" cards at home or at the office. Send one along periodically for no special reason. And how about sharing a cartoon?

• When a copy of the current pro or college football schedule (or that of the symphony or theater) falls into your hands, make copies and attach your business card. Send the schedule along to friends with a note that says, "Thought of you when I got this schedule. Just in case you haven't located a copy yet..."

• When a special brochure or catalog falls into your hands, drop it in the mail with this note: "Thought of your beautifully decorated apartment when I got this catalog—see anything of interest?"

Better yet, have an assistant do the above. When you read an article you find thought-provoking, jot a note to your assistant at the top of the page: "Clip and send a copy to Tom Gerrard, Susan Courtney, and Mark White."

Staying in touch, though important, doesn't necessarily have to cost much time.

13. Use Margin Notes for Replies

But what will people think about such an informal response? They'll think you're a busy person who wants to get them a fast answer.

On what occasions are informal notes in the margin appropriate? On almost any occasion. I've seen the highest-level executives write margin notes to each other on formal research reports, on major client proposals, on letters to clients, and certainly on internal memos. What more direct, clear, thorough way to communicate than on the document itself, where all related queries and responses cannot possibly be separated?

If you need a copy of your response jotted in the margin, copy the original document and your note before you return it.

Think fast. Think informal.

14. Use "Stamped" Replies

Although "everybody else does it" is never a sound reason for doing anything except eating and bathing, stamped replies have become very acceptable in almost all arenas—private industry, governmental agencies, and certainly for family matters.

How many of these stamped messages have you received?

Your payment has been received. Thank you.

Your payment has not yet been received. Would you please phone us at once.

This is not a bill. Do not send payment. This form has been forwarded simply as information about action taken with regard to your account.

Your membership will expire in 60 days.

Your letter has been received in our office and routed to the appropriate department for action. You will hear from us within 14 days.

Your proposal has been received. Thank you for responding so promptly. We will give your proposal careful attention, and you may expect a formal decision shortly.

Your recent check included an overpayment of $14.59. We will apply that amount toward your next monthly payment unless we hear from you to do otherwise.

We are enclosing the information you requested. Someone will phone you shortly.

Thank you for your phone call. To avoid delay, we are sending your information on its way with this brief note.

Whatever the message, consider a stamp. Two strokes—one on the ink pad, the other on the paper— and you're in business.

15. Pay Bills Only Twice a Month; File Receipts Immediately

Time-and-motion studies assure us that we waste a certain amount of time just getting started on a task—deciding when, what, and how to do something, as well as gathering ourselves and materials to do the project. Bill paying is no exception.

Pay bills in a systematic, not random, way. Toss bills into a file or other designated drawer or container as they arrive. Then every two weeks, assemble envelopes, stamps, checkbook, receipt files, and write your checks. Yes, due dates on invoices vary. But if you write checks systematically every two weeks, you'll find that you meet all payment deadlines.

That is not to say, however, that you should *mail* all these newly written checks immediately. If your two-week plan catches a bill on the day it arrives and the bill says you have another thirty days to make payment, fine. Write the check, stuff it in the envelope ready to mail, and then jot the due date in tiny print just above the stamp. Hold on to the checks that don't need to be mailed immediately. That way, you keep your money in your own account, earning interest up to the last moment, and still have the efficiency of the twice-a-month system. Place the payment envelopes in a holder in order of their due dates and check the holder each day for those that need to be dropped in the mail.

Then if you suddenly decide to leave town for a few days or a few weeks, there's no last-minute dilemma about scrambling to pay the bills before you go or leaving them and risking past-due penalties upon your return.

And about those receipts: Mark files "utilities," "insurance," "car loan," and so forth and drop the receipts into them as soon as you finish writing checks—not into a "to-be-filed-later" drawer. The extra one or two minutes the filing takes now may save you hours later as you search to see if you've paid a bill twice or indeed skipped a payment as some creditor may mistakenly insist.

Treat your personal check-writing system as seriously as your business system.

16. Dictate Instructions, Speeches, and First Drafts of Long Documents

The average person speaks about six times faster than he or she writes by longhand. Therefore, it stands to reason that "paperwork by mouth" is faster than paperwork by hand. (For advantages of using computers, see the next tip.)

What keeps most people from trying to dictate is a lack of confidence in their dictating skills—often based on only one or two efforts at dictating the wrong things in the wrong manner.

To be effective in dictating, you have to prepare and practice. An off-the-top-of-the-head dictating session usually results in a scrambled first draft that takes just as much time to edit in longhand as it would have taken if the first draft had been written in longhand to begin with. The results of a dictated document are directly proportional to the thinking that has gone on beforehand.

Whether a few notes jotted on a notepad or a formal outline, a dictator needs a plan to dictate a document that's well organized and needs only minor editing to become a final draft.

The second consideration in dictating effectively is to match the task to the method. In other words, dictation is most useful for tasks such as giving extensive instructions to staff members, drafting speeches, and composing long reports.

Instructions: Good instructions mean thorough instructions. When you start to write instructions by longhand and the task becomes time-consuming, the tendency is to omit more and more detail, just providing the basic steps.

The real possibility for error, however, lies in the details. What seems obvious to the instruction-giver is not always obvious to the doer. Therefore, simply by talking the instructions in such a fast method, you tend to add more explanation, resulting in more thorough instructions. It's also a good idea to give complex instructions "live" to others so that they can ask for clarification. The dictating equipment becomes simply a recorder. If a question comes up later about completing the task, the dictation becomes the backup.

Speeches: Dictation particularly improves speech-writing because a draft sounds much more conversational when spoken rather than written. The word choice tends to be informal and rhythmic, the sentences shorter, and the tone more colloquial—all goals that speechwriters strive for.

Long Reports: Dictating a long report carries a psychological advantage. Part of the difficulty in writing results from procrastination, from getting started on what seems like an overwhelming task. The sheer speed at which you can attack an overwhelming, time-intensive task gives you a psychological advantage. You can talk a two-to-three-hundred-page document into a recorder in a matter of eight to sixteen hours. Then just having "something on paper" to work with moves you into the editing phase of writing—a much easier task for most people. With a draft in hand, you envision yourself on the downside of the hill.

Effective dictation involves both appropriate preparation and tasks. Choose an appropriate task (instructions, speeches, long reports), and prepare an outline of your ideas. Talk your thoughts into the recorder. Then take your time editing.

17. Compose Your Own Short Documents on the Computer

Personal computers have allowed us to combine the best of both worlds—the speed of dictating and the ease of reviewing documents on a printed page. Like dictation, composing on the computer allows you to get your ideas down much more quickly than when writing in longhand. The added benefit of the computer screen is seeing how long your paragraphs are, where you need to break them, how complex sentences are, and where bulleted lists would be most effective. Your eye works with your brain in determining structure and layout.

Some professionals once considered computers appropriate only for lower-level employees. But nowadays, computer-literate people can compose a document themselves on the computer more quickly than they can explain their intentions to someone else.

After composing, you can then turn the document over to an assistant for the final touches: adding the address, running the spellchecker, paginating.

If your goal is to compose something quickly, writing it yourself may make more sense than explaining what you want to someone else, seeing his effort, editing his effort, reexplaining where he went wrong, and rereading what he revises for you a second and third time.

Composing on the computer allows you to see the final version as it evolves in your thought process. The result is often a better document.

18. Eliminate Meaningless Documentation of Phone Conversations

Some people would profit if they knew their phones were being bugged. That way, they could forget the nuisance of writing a longhand version of the phone conversation "for the files."

Do you feel compelled to write a recap of a conversation because you don't trust your own memory or that of the other person? Or, do you just want proof that if something goes wrong, you aren't to blame for the foul-up?

On occasion, either reason is justifiable—the downside of a quick call is not having a written record. But before you document phone conversations, ask yourself what you'll do if the other person misunderstands. Are you going to pull out your file and say, "See there, you're the one who fouled up"? If not, the situation still comes down to whose memory or recollection of the conversation is correct. A file copy of the details of the situation does nothing to prove who is right; it simply proves you remember the conversation one way and someone else remembers it differently.

If you want to confirm details *for yourself*, just make a brief note that you talked about x, y, and z on such and such date and drop it in your file.

Where the other person is concerned, either the phone call or the written confirmation is unnecessary. Make it one or the other.

19. Eliminate Most Cover Letters

Approximately one-fourth of all letters and memos are transmittals for reports, proposals, or other routine inquiries for information. And most of these transmittals routinely go to the same person weekly, monthly, or quarterly. In other words, they're boilerplate documents that the receiver could read in her sleep.

Why not send them?

• They're superfluous. Most simply say, "I'm sending you something. You now have it in your hands."

• They're ignored. When people recognize them as a form letter, they don't read them anyway. And if you slip in a new sentence of explanation somewhere about the action readers are supposed to take, they'll miss that sentence.

• They're repetitious. Most repeat what the attached document says.

- They often contradict and confuse. If the writer includes a good summary in the cover letter but doesn't word that message exactly the same way as in the attached report, the reader becomes confused about the different summary statements.
- They delay action. How much faster it would be to stick the requested information in an envelope and send it on its way without waiting for a convenient time to prepare the cover letter.

If you need a record of submission, simply put a "Submitted to..." and "Submitted by..." along with the date on the title page.

In responding to customers, add a more personal touch with a note on your business card clipped to the brochure or other information. They'll appreciate your speed in reply and your personal involvement in the response.

When you need cover letters as a sales tool—to make a point about the enclosed document or to tempt the reader to keep reading the brochure or proposal—use them. But for the most part, transmittals serve little purpose.

20. Squelch the Urge to Confirm Everything in Writing

Whatever happened to the handshake to close a deal? For some it has gone the way of the horse and buggy; for others, it's still much in vogue. I deal with insurance agents who say "you're covered" over the phone and have paid claims when things still hadn't been put in writing. I, as well as others, have distributed big-ticket items without having distribution agreements in writing. I've bought, sold, leased, and "unleased" real estate without having agreements in writing—or blood. And I don't think my experience is unusual.

Your ability to size people up comes into use here. Most people have a gut feeling about those they can depend on and those who will squirm in times of adversity.

So before you take the time to confirm everything in writing, ask yourself these questions:

- Is your memory or theirs that bad?
- Are you going to phone again with all the details anyway?
- Will confirmation make both parties feel better about the agreement?
- Will confirmation create distrust and suspicion about the agreement and the relationship?

- What's the worst that can happen if this confirmation is not on paper?
- Will the confirmation speed up or slow down the action?
- If this is confirmed on paper and the other party tries to back out, what measures *could* you take to enforce the agreement?
- If this is confirmed on paper and the other party tries to back out, what measures *would* you take to enforce the agreement?

If after you've scrutinized the situation with these questions and you still think a confirmation is in order, then follow these guidelines for making the one you write accomplish its purpose:

First, put the summary of what you're writing to confirm up front in the letter or memo. This confirmation is the bottom-line message of interest.

Second, repeat all details of the situation: date, time, place, enclosures, amounts, qualifying statements, promises. In short, don't rely on any previous oral or written information. Repetition of details is the main purpose of the written confirmation.

Third, be sure to mention the date or manner of any initial phone, personal, or written contract/ agreement/meeting/request.

Fourth, unless obvious or routine, suggest how the recipient should contact you in case the confirmation reveals some error or misunderstanding.

Finally, provide signature lines for both parties.

One last check: If you continue to get follow-up questions about your confirmations and continue to change the details and working arrangements despite the written document, think again about the real need for the confirmation in future dealings. You probably still should be talking rather than writing.

21. Eliminate Most Trip Reports

The most natural thing in the world to do after you return from a trip is to tell your boss, colleague, or client what you found out. When asked, "How was your trip?" you usually tell the gist of it in a sentence or two.

Why then force yourself to put all this information in a formal report? Most of the time simply because "it's always been done that way before." When you commit things to a formal report, you tend to throw in unnecessary information that requires extra writing time and extra reading time for all concerned.

You state the purpose of the trip, what you were

trying to accomplish, the date of each event on your travel itinerary, who accompanied you, how you got there, the agenda for the visit, and all the other unnecessary detail that obscures the key information: the significance of the trip.

Only the "meat" of the information should go in such a required report anyway. And if decision makers take action based on your first, immediate oral trip report, why put the rest in writing at all?

22. Eliminate Computer Printouts of Uninterpretable Information

The computer has not created the paperless office; it has simply proliferated paper throughout the organization. With the touch of a key, you can send copies to the world and can multiply your number-crunching efforts to an infinite degree.

But for all the most computer-callused employees, computer printouts look like Sanskrit. Most readers find the uninterpreted, unabridged printout of numbers about as appealing as the index at the back of most books.

Numbers rarely speak for themselves; they need to be interpreted. Likewise, with a computer printout—the numbers, charts, and graphs rarely speak for themselves. They have to be interpreted to be usable in the typical business environment. Therefore, they should be summarized, not served up raw.

23. Eliminate Weekly/ Monthly Activity Reports

So what's the problem with activity reports? You have to sacrifice time for "doing" in order to write about your "doing."

With an arbitrary rule that employees will prepare activity reports for certain periods of time, the tendency is to manufacture things to report. Certainly, the lack of activity doesn't show up on anyone's periodic report. Employees just strain for items to include—they can always exaggerate the length of time a project required, be vague in their activities, or obscure the insignificance of their accomplishments.

Activity reports rarely tell a supervisor how employees have been spending their time. There's often no correlation whatsoever between accomplishments and time spent on a particular activity.

For organizations that require "activity" reports for highlights of what employees have *accomplished*, that's another story altogether.

The best reporting procedure requires people to report on projects at certain specified stages. When the projects are delegated, bosses identify the significant phases of the project and determine report-back times. Only when something unusual occurs should you bring that "surprise" to someone's attention. Formal written reports on day-to-day, routine matters waste everybody's time.

So what if you're working in an organization or in a department that requires such routine weekly or monthly reports?

Point out to your management the sameness of your reports and the time you spend in preparing them. Then suggest "exception" reporting. Tell your bosses you'll complete a report whenever something's "not routine." And then do so. They'll come to trust your judgment about what they need or want to know in written form.

24. Eliminate Duplicate Information Submitted in Multiple Formats

Does this ritual sound familiar? Employees at the lowest level report the numbers to their bosses—how many accounts they've called on, how many sales they've made, how many plant sites they've visited. The bosses, in turn, select the highlights of those reports to compile for their reports to the regional directors. The regional directors then condense the key data from the group directors and put the information in their regional reports. The regional executive then reshuffles the data into still another report passed on to the vice president.

In most corporations computers crunch and reformat numbers in innumerable ways. Look for those duplicate compilations that maybe don't take *you* long to toss aside or throw in the file but that have taken others a long time to compile.

If you're caught in such a regurgitation ritual, find a better way. Locate the necessary information in its current format and either highlight it, put a gummed note on it, bullet it, or circle it in red, and pass it along with a note that says, "Here's the information you asked for. I've not *delayed* my response to reformat this information in still another formal report."

See if most people won't accept the already reported and interpreted data for their use without requiring you to recompile it into yet another format.

25. Eliminate Minutes for Most Meetings

When you conduct a meeting with all members present, rarely is there a need for minutes. No one reads them; they're simply typed and filed away.

Later, if someone fails to carry through on his or her assigned task and you want to place blame, someone at the meeting always remembers without the aid of written minutes.

Only for absent staff members do minutes at a routine staff meeting become important. On those occasions, consider recording the meeting and sending absentees the cassette. As they listen, they get the whole gist of the discussion. Yes, listening to the entire recorded meeting will be more time-consuming than reading minutes, but then that method may encourage everyone to be present at the next scheduled meeting.

For most meetings, if you want a record of what

was discussed, the agenda sent out with the meeting announcement can also serve as that record. On that hard copy, jot any follow-up action and the responsible person by the pertinent agenda item. Or, where appropriate, add a statement of the conclusions beside an agenda item. This annotated agenda will serve the purpose of minutes for all but the most formal meetings.

26. Ask Why When *Anyone* Requests a Report; Suggest Alternatives

People assign reports for many different reasons:

- "You don't look busy; here's something for you to do. I've got to have something to show my boss to prove that we're doing something over here."
- "Leave me alone; I'm interested in something else now. Why don't you go write a report on..."
- "I don't know enough about what you're trying to tell me to discuss it with you; educate me and then I'll let you know if it's worth pursuing."

- "This cost a lot of money; we need a report to show for it."
- "You're on to a good idea [or meaningful information]; I'd like to follow that up. When you write the report,...?"

The interpretation for the line "Why don't you put together a report on that?" ranges from the positive to the negative.

Whatever the reason people ask for reports—whether they're just trying to keep you busy or they think that's the only way to stay informed—ask why before you comply.

When they give a weak answer, offer an alternative: "Did you know that those numbers you're asking me for are already available in the x, y, z document?" "Did you know we could get you a computer printout of those numbers, which is essentially what you want—you'll have the information this afternoon if we don't have to put it in a formal report." Or, "Why don't I pull that information together and put it in a visual so you can really see graphically the variations? Would that be sufficient?"

You'd be surprised how many times people will accept your shortcut. They just have a habit of asking for a report when all they want is a piece of information, a brief list, a summary, or a graphic representation of the key numbers or issues.

Both you and the recipient will save writing and reading time.

27. Use Idea Wheels for To-Do Lists

To-do lists, of course, keep us on target and on time. But many people can't find their desktops for to-do lists scattered everywhere. And then there's always the matter of those lists becoming so out of order and messy with markouts that valuable time is spent just copying them over.

(For those of you who make such lists just for the pleasure of scratching through finished items, forget this tip. There are more sinful ways to spend your time than worrying about this timewaster.)

Try the idea wheel structure for to-dos—a structure that can easily accommodate a day's worth of surprises and priority changes. Start with a circle in the center of your page to represent the hub of the wheel; then add spokes for your currently known to-dos. As the day progresses, reorganize by project, place, event, time, or person—depending on use. Number the spokes according to priority and go to work.

Two samples follow.

Use Idea Wheels for To-Do Lists
To-Do Idea Wheel—by Person

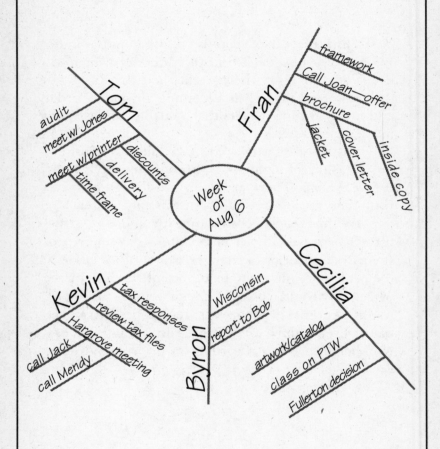

Week of Aug 6

Tom: audit, meet w/ Jones, meet w/printer, discounts, delivery, time frame

Fran: framework, Call Joan—offer, brochure, jacket, cover letter, inside copy

Kevin: tax responses, review tax files, Hargrove meeting, call Jack, call Mendy

Byron: Wisconsin, report to Bob

Cecilia: artwork/catalog, class on PTW, Fullerton decision

Note: You can always number the spokes according to priority.

Use Idea Wheels for To-Do Lists
To-Do Idea Wheel—by Place

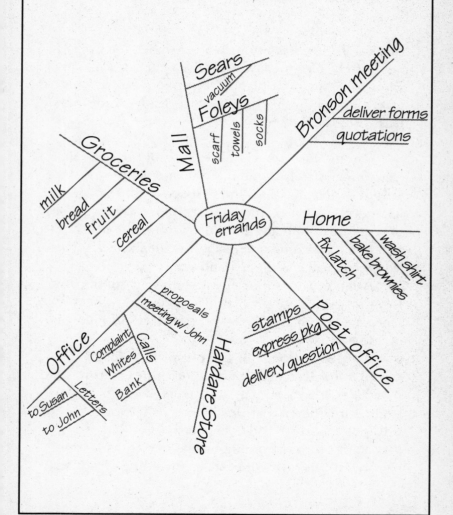

28. Use Idea Wheels for Project Planning

(For the basic concept of the idea wheel, see tip 27.)

Rarely do you know all the steps in a project when you begin to plan. The project evolves—one task leads to the next task, which leads to the next task. All the better to see the entire framework before you begin.

Use the idea wheel to break down the steps that come immediately to mind. For example, record step 1, step 2, and step 3 on the first spokes of the wheel. Then try to break those tasks into substeps. The process will gradually unfold in complete detail. If not, and if you omit a key step, the idea wheel always leaves room for additions and revisions.

After you have the major steps and substeps in front of you, use this project-planning wheel to delegate specific subtasks or projects. Add names beside each spoke.

Also, at this stage of the planning, refer to your calendar to determine and record interim completion dates for each step. In this format, it's easy to begin with the crucial deadline on the project and work backward toward each step.

This project-planning wheel serves as a brief picture of the overall project, including deadlines and people assigned to each step. You can then issue a copy of the complete process to everyone involved so that the left hand knows what the right hand is doing and how missed deadlines affect the overall success of the project.

29. Use Idea Wheels for Problem Analysis and Decision Making

(For the basic concept of the idea wheel, see tip 27.)

Do you waste time and paperwork looking at the pros and cons of a decision? Our analysis of tasks and our decisions profit from our committing them to paper—but not a lot of paper, not a long report, not scrambled half thoughts to ourselves. The idea wheel replaces the time-honored list of pros and cons, of dos and don'ts.

Once you put things on an idea wheel and think from problem to solution, or symptom to cause, you'll focus your thinking in a very succinct, powerful way.

Save such paper because when you begin to rethink your decision two days later, you can retrace and verify your assumptions and conclusions.

Use Idea Wheels for Project Planning

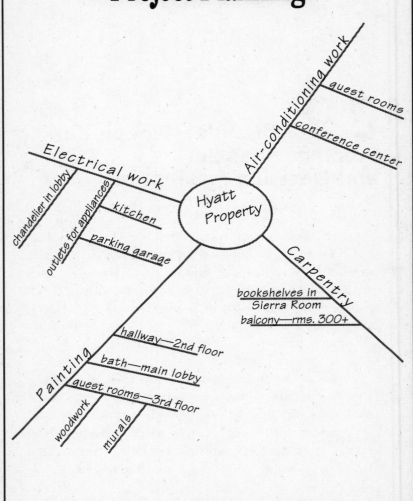

Air-conditioning work
- guest rooms
- conference center

Electrical work
- chandelier in lobby
- outlets for appliances
- kitchen
- parking garage

Hyatt Property

Carpentry
- bookshelves in Sierra Room
- balcony—rms. 300+

Painting
- hallway—2nd floor
- bath—main lobby
- guest rooms—3rd floor
- woodwork
- murals

Use Idea Wheels for Problem Analysis and Decision Making

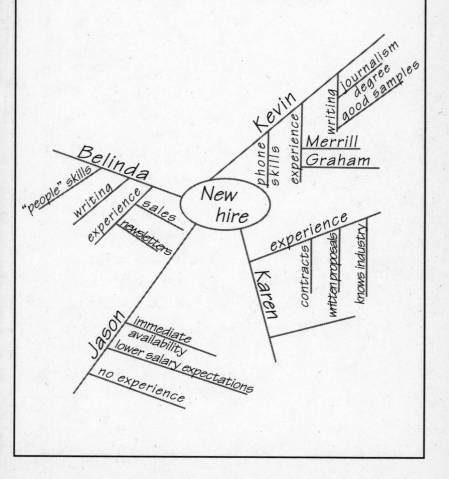

Use Idea Wheels for Problem-Analysis and Decision Making

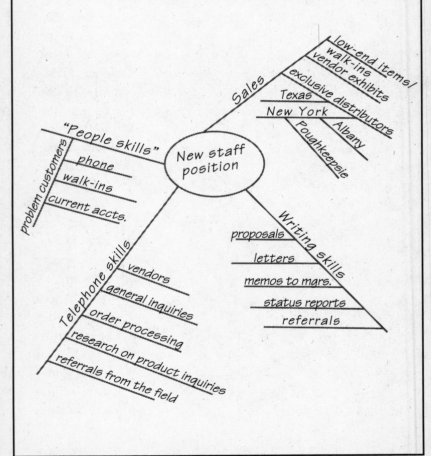

30. Use Idea Wheels for Meeting Agendas and Assignments

(For the basic concept of the idea wheel, see tip 27.)

Do you work with people who always seem to get meetings off target? People who are always bringing up ideas that need to be decided . . . sometime? Those with hidden agendas that encourage arguing rather than moving forward in a meeting?

If so, the idea wheel as an "evolving" agenda may be the answer to the problem. On a flip chart, sketch an idea wheel for each issue you want to discuss. Add spokes for facts or questions beside each discussion topic.

In the meeting's opening moments, give attendees an overview by directing them to the flip chart. Ask whether they have topics to add and put their suggestions on the evolving agenda at that point.

During the meeting when someone starts to get off target with, "Oh, by the way, while we're on this subject, we also need to discuss . . ." you have a formal structure to add the idea to the agenda.

You can comfortably respond, "That's a good point. That issue would be appropriate when we get into spoke four." Then add the topic to the chart

Use Idea Wheels for Meeting Agendas and Assignments

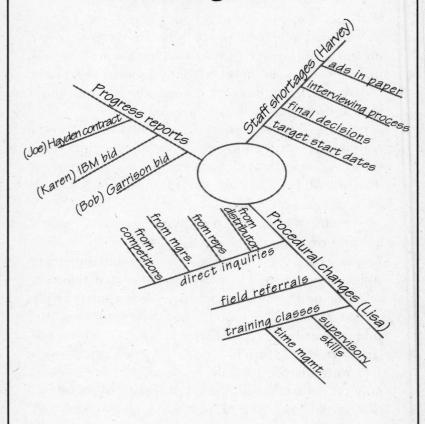

Staff shortages (Harvey)
- ads in paper
- interviewing process
- final decisions
- target start dates

Progress reports
- (Joe) Hayden contract
- (Karen) IBM bid
- (Bob) Garrison bid

Procedural changes (Lisa)
- direct inquiries
  - from competitors
  - from mgrs.
  - from reps
  - from distributor
- field referrals
- training classes
  - supervisory skills
  - time mgmt.

wheel while they watch; they'll feel assured that you'll return to that matter.

The idea wheel agenda also eliminates the need for meeting minutes. As you discuss each issue, put a check mark by it. There's rarely a need to record conclusions. If you make assignments for follow-up actions, jot names beside the appropriate agenda items.

If you must have a written record of the meeting, you can always cram the flip chart pages in a drawer for posterity.

31. Use Idea Wheels to Record Client Conversations

(For the basic concept of the idea wheel, see tip 27.)

How many times have you been in a meeting with two or three decision makers or buyers trying to tell you all at once what they want in your proposal or report?

How do most of us cope with this information overload? We grab the old yellow legal pad and take copious notes—six, seven, eight pages of scribbled phrases, sentences, and other tidbits. Then when we get back to our office, we intend to summarize what was said in the meeting so we can prepare a thorough report, proposal, bid, or letter.

What's more, in reading through the six or seven pages, we discover our notes are terribly disorganized and even unintelligible. For example, we see "$68,000" scribbled in the margin. Now was $68,000 what management said the first bidder had estimated for labor? Or was that what the group said the budget was? Did they say they wanted to spend $68,000 over the next three years, or just the first year?

The next note says simply "safety." Was the client talking about safety related to equipment? Safety because of governmental regulations? Safety in the testing procedures? How does safety relate to all these other ideas? Most of us don't take good notes when we're trying to write *and* listen.

Another reason for such disorder: People don't speak in an orderly fashion in a meeting. In fact, they "talk over" each other and carry on side conversations as well.

To solve the note-taking problem, try the idea wheel for meeting conversations.

Draw your idea wheel as the meeting begins. Put the first issue that's brought up inside the first wheel; add the spokes as people bring up different points, facts, questions, or issues. If they change topics, flip the page, make a new idea wheel, and organize those ideas separately. If they then go back to the first

Use Idea Wheels to Record Client Conversations

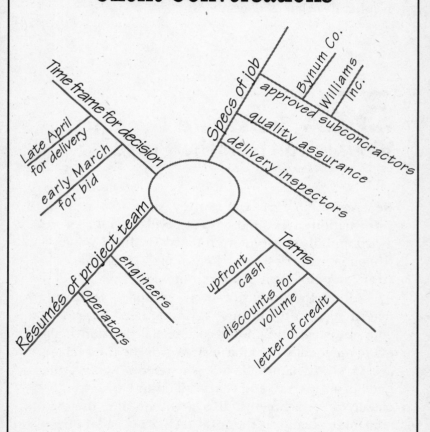

Time frame for decision
Late April for delivery
early March for bid

Specs of job
Bynum Co.
Williams Inc.
approved subconcractors
quality assurance
delivery inspectors

Résumés of project team
engineers
operators

Terms
upfront cash
discounts for volume
letter of credit

topic, flip back to the first wheel and add the information.

When you walk out of that client or boss's office, you'll have an organized picture of your meeting conversation—without spending two hours in your car, at the airport, or in your office deciphering cryptic, disorganized scribbles.

32. Substitute Dynamic Visuals for Lengthy Prose

Be creative in how you convey your information. Information presented visually will be quicker to grasp and also have more impact. In this TV age, a fifteen- or thirty-second high-impact spot makes a stronger point than a two-minute editorial.

Although you're not always trying to sell products or services to customers, you do need to present your information or ideas to internal decision makers in an equally dynamic way. Words, by themselves, are rarely dynamic. That's the reason we feel the need in a report to add charts, diagrams, or graphs—usually as attachments. But when we add them as attachments, all but the most technical readers treat them as footnotes, disregarding their helpfulness in zeroing in on the real facts and numbers.

Therefore, I suggest that you do away with the lengthy prose altogether and put all the key information on the graphic, chart, or diagram itself. With software that makes colorful graphics possible by the touch of a keystroke, your message will be easy to grasp and far more memorable than paragraphs of prose.

Visuals ensure that your information gets the attention it deserves. So the next time you're asked for a "report" on some subject, start with a visual of the key information. Only if the reader asks for more should you return to the old prose report format.

33. Use, but Don't Abuse, Electronic Message Systems

If you have an electronic mail system, you know its usefulness and speed in conveying messages. And those two facts likewise represent the downside of electronic mail—informality that leads to carelessness, disorganization, and clarity problems.

Forget the Prose; Substitute a Visual

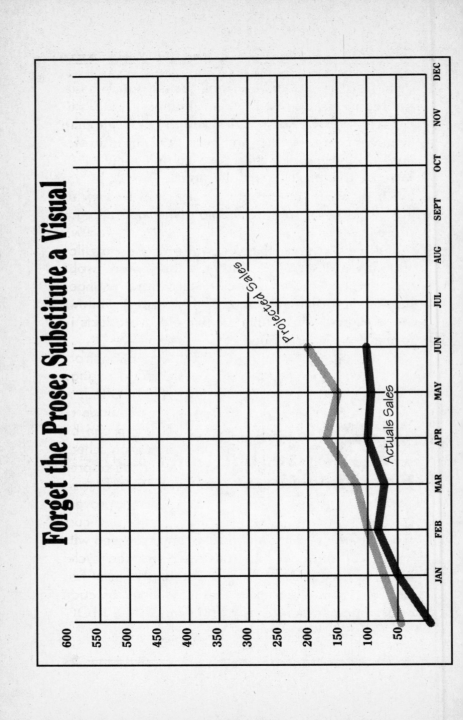

Avoid a "brain dump" communication that causes the need for three or four additional interactions to clear up the confusion. Because the electronic mail system is so informal, people tend to compose *as they think*. For example:

> Subject: Support and Control Review
> Carl, I am in the process of arranging a Support and Control Review (SCR) for two products well in advance of their availability date (12/16—) to correct any problems or implement any needed changes recommended by the CPA firm(s). Follow-on SCRs for the six remaining products in the family need to be done by 4/—.
> I have obtained an authorization from Bob Smith, the XYZ Controller, to engage the CPA firm(s) so we can get started. A key aspect involves writing a definition of the work scope so that (1) a firm can be selected and a cost and completion schedule can be determined, and (2) an appropriation containing that work scope/cost/schedule can be written and approved. Because of the closeness of the first customer ship (availability) dates coupled with the time required to complete the cycle, time is very critical. One program has approximately one million lines of code and the other around two hundred KLOC.

These products cannot be shipped without satisfying the SCR requirement.

Because of the critical time factors, I have recommended to the development team that Vendor ABC be used to conduct the SCR because of OP's experience in doing SCRs and their overall familiarity with banking applications. FYI, OP is Oliver Perry Auditors (from whom we are acquiring the products). I have already gotten a clearance from CD-Taylor Business Controls to use them. Do you have a problem in using a single source? If so, what other justification do I need in addition to what I have already indicated?

If the work had to be put out to bid for three firms, what is the process and what amount of time would likely be required from start to finish in awarding the work? How do I arrange to get a firm in to define the objective and provide a sufficient work statement?

What do you require to get started? Please give me a call.

You see what I mean? Questions among actions. Details thrown in randomly. Requests buried among facts.

To make electronic mail both quick and effective, think *before* you write. Organize your thinking, and then give a brief summary of your main point/ message at the beginning. Second, tell the reader what action or response you want from him or her. *Then* go into details or elaboration.

This arrangement allows readers to look at the first screen and make one of four decisions immediately: Read now? Read later? Route elsewhere? Discard?

Make sure your opening message and requests/ recommendations invite the reader's immediate response. Informal, electronic communication should not mean careless or unfocused messages. If you have to send a second message to interpret the first, what time have you saved?

Think *before* you write, not *as* you write. (For more information about the MADE format, see tip 43.)

34. Find out What Goes Where and Why; Stop Sending the Unnecessary

Do you ever get the impression that you're doing things just because they've always been done that way? All paper is not created equal, nor are all

Worksheet: Paper Audit—What Goes Where and Why?
Incoming Documents (Reports, Correspondence, Forms, Printouts)

Title	What Do You Do with It?	Why?	Could You Do without It?	Alternatives for Conveying Information?

Worksheet: Paper Audit—What Goes Where and Why?
Outgoing Documents (Reports, Correspondence, Forms, Printouts)

Title	What Do You Do with It?	Why?	Could You Stop Sending It?	Is Information Available Elsewhere?

requests created equal. Begin to question every piece of paper that you handle. When a document comes to you to review, analyze, add to, respond to, approve, or pass on, ask yourself: Where does this go and why?

Do a paper audit. Trace the paper trail for both incoming and outgoing documents (see preceding tables) to find out what goes where and why. You may discover that the reasons for some paperwork or procedures have long disappeared. Although this audit requires a little paperwork initially, eventually you will identify duplication of effort, unnecessary procedures, redundant reports, and duplicate forms. Eliminate the duplicate and the unnecessary.

35. Reconsider the Idea, "I Can Do It Better/Faster Myself."

Some paperwork you can do better and faster yourself. For example, it takes you less time to write a brief, handwritten note or fill in three lines on a form than it takes you to write instructions to tell someone else how or why to do the task for you.

But don't get carried away with this concept. Be

cautious of bogging yourself down in excessive paperwork simply because you don't trust another person to be as detailed, as accurate, as concerned, or as fast as you are. Identify and hire those detail-oriented people who are committed to helping you with your paperwork.

Here are clues to their detail orientation. Either make some observations yourself or ask job applicants questions that focus on this penchant for detail:

- Résumés and correspondence without typos and spelling or grammatical errors
- Those who insist that their checkbooks balance to the penny
- Those who can name the authors of their favorite books
- Those who can rattle off their driver's license number
- Those who can tell you how many college credit hours they took in each subject

Surround yourself with detail-oriented people and then trust them to do what needs to be done without always "making sure that it's done right" by doing it yourself.

36. Delegate Effectively— with Full Authority and Clear Instructions

Is your desk always piled high with memos, letters, or reports waiting for your approval signature on some action? If so, you may be creating your own burdensome paperwork by improperly delegating tasks.

Subordinates or peers working with you as teammates on a particular project may feel the constant need to "report back" on any action taken or to seek your approval before they take any action whatsoever.

Rethink your delegating manner. Here are guidelines to minimize unnecessary report-backs and paperwork steps:

- Outline to the person the end result of the task you want accomplished.
- Suggest one or several approaches *if you want to*, and be honest about whether you want people to follow your plan of action exactly. Be clear about whether they have a choice in how they get things done.
- Give them the parameters of the project— completion date, budget, available resources, and so forth.

- Tell them at what point you want check-backs. Upon completion of certain interim tasks? By a certain date? Routinely every week? (Are you sure?) If the expense goes over a certain dollar amount? If they have problems with x or y? If they expect a delay? If they can't get z to happen?
- Let them know that oral check-backs are okay—a phone call or a conversation in the hall with you.

Once you've effectively delegated a task, step out of the way. Let others do their assigned tasks with the full authority you've delegated and without the accompanying paperwork that constant report-backs involve.

37. Work Ahead of Deadlines

"I work better under pressure." Most people do *not* work better under pressure—they only work faster. That's simply the lie people tell themselves when they procrastinate.

What procrastinators mean by that statement, of course, is that the pressure forces them to focus on the job and "do something" even if it's wrong. But the deadline pressure doesn't mean that they do the job effectively and efficiently. Under pressure to meet a deadline, they don't have enough time to check for accuracy, to allow a cool-off period for analysis of their efforts, or to check for gaps in logic or for missing information.

If you still believe the "I work better under pressure" myth, think how many times you've completed a project only to have your eyes pop open at 2:00 A.M., three days later: "I should have added... It's too bad that document's already gone out."

Objectivity about your work comes with time. The only way to allow that objectivity is to work ahead of schedule. Do your best paperwork the first time around and then move ahead to another task while your subconscious works on what you've just completed. Later, come back and review your first efforts.

When you work down to the deadline under pressure, you make errors. And then you redo, and redo, and redo. That's unnecessary paperwork when you least have the time.

38. Use Deadlines to Your Benefit and to Motivate Yourself to Better Work

You don't do your best work under pressure—that is, pressure exerted by some external force. But if you create your own *early* deadlines, you can often motivate yourself to set up a realistic schedule of work.

If you have several paperwork projects, don't wait until you feel the "inspiration" to do them all. Instead, look at your calendar and pace yourself just as if you were a marathon runner. Give yourself some deadlines as to when each of the documents/projects have to be done—and stick with them. You'll do a more thorough job on each project because you have more time on each and more energy and attention to focus.

The principle is the same as that expressed with the cliché, "Obviously, this lemon of a car was built on a Friday." Don't let your paperwork read as though it all were done between 3:00 P.M. and 5:00 P.M. on Friday.

39. Create a Climate of Trust to Eliminate Self-Protective Writing

"As we discussed...," "pursuant to our discussion...," "as you requested...," "to follow up our telephone conversation...": if your documents and those of your colleagues are sprinkled with these phrases, chances are there's little trust among you.

In our past research within corporations, we frequently asked, "What kind of documents do you write that you think could be eliminated?" We anticipated answers such as activity reports, trip reports, monthly status reports, or any number of other particular organizational reports. What the overwhelming majority mentioned, however, was "CYA reports." People generate paperwork upward, laterally, and downward simply to cover themselves in case there's a problem. They want to "go on record."

So what can you do in your corner of the world?

Let people know they can trust you. If you say you're going to call, call. If you say you're going to do something, do it. If you say you're going to act, act. Once you build up a bank account of trust, bosses, peers, and customers won't always demand that you keep them informed in writing.

Second, stifle the urge to blame others when

things go wrong. Instead, focus on the corrective action. The attention to solution rather than blame will go a long way in stifling others' urges to "put it in writing" where you're concerned.

40. Consider the Cost and Time in Double-Checking

In addition to taking risks about what to save, take risks about what to verify. Some people spend hours verifying and confirming data when their effort is far more costly than any mistake they may uncover.

For example, an accounting clerk in our office once spent almost four hours sorting duplicates of photos we'd had printed in mass and then matching the negative number on each to the photographer's invoice. Why? She thought he'd sent us a duplicate invoice for two prints. Four hours later, she verified that he had indeed overcharged us $5.76. At her $8-an-hour salary, she spent $32 to catch a $5.76 error.

Be aware of the cost of double-checking. Some mistakes cost more to uncover and correct than the undetected errors themselves cost. Make sure your checks-and-balances systems really *save* rather than *cost* money.

41. Aim to Do It Right the First Time

Many people use paperwork as a thinking process. For example, they fill out a form in pencil just to make sure they have the right information. Once they finish the form and determine that, indeed, they do have all the information, they hand it to someone else to "redo" in ink or type—or worse yet, redo it themselves.

Why take any document and pencil notes or thoughts in the margin because you're not sure that you're going to raise the right questions or that your editing marks are not exactly correct? Once you get to the end of the document, you find that you've done things appropriately the first time but that your notes aren't formal. So what do you do? Go back and redo?

Aim to do things right the first time. Don't let yourself get caught thinking, "Oh, well, I'll just take a stab at this the first time around. I'll redo it better later."

You're doubling your paperwork efforts with such an approach. Be thorough, accurate, and precise the first time around.

42. Develop a Personal Information Card for Recurring Questions

Keep frequently needed information at your fingertips by developing an index card, file card, or fact sheet on every member of your family (or staff).

Record some or all of the following items, as necessary:

- driver's license numbers
- Social Security numbers
- group insurance numbers and filing addresses
- bank account numbers
- dates of birthdays, marriage and employment anniversaries, divorces
- school telephone numbers
- business credit card numbers
- employee identification numbers

- doctors' names and numbers
- prescription numbers

Of course, to compile such a list at the outset would be a time-consuming chore. Instead, compile the list on an "as you go" basis. Every time you have to fill out a form or report that requires this kind of data, jot the item on the card or fact sheet. Within about six months' time, you'll have a full data sheet on everyone in your family (or on your staff).

Keeping these vital facts, names, and numbers together so that you don't have to research and collect them over and over for each new task reduces paperwork time considerably.

43. Use the MADE Format for Delivering All Phone, In-Person, and Written Messages

Do you tire of hearing once-upon-a-time stories in your day-to-day life? How about phone calls or letters that begin, "Hello, my name is David Sojo. Ed Smith suggested that I call you about the Friday afternoon meeting. He was in Miami last week and ran into Lisa Borden, and over dinner they began to talk about the issue of..."

Pretty soon, you're ready to scream, "Get to the point!"

Keep that sentiment in mind every time you start a conversation or letter. Your reader or listener is saying, "Get to the point. Then I'll know if I want to listen or read further and which details I need to pay attention to."

Use the MADE format to help you present your information in a succinct, clearly organized way that will reduce time in writing, reading, speaking, and understanding messages. The MADE format can be applied to communication in all forms—letters, reports, proposals, conversations, electronic mail, and oral presentations.

M Message
What is the bottom-line message of interest to your reader?

A Action
What action do you plan to take next based on this message? Or, what action do you want the reader to take?

D Details
Elaborate on the necessary details: who, when, where, why, how, or how much?

E Evidence
Mention any attachments or enclosures.

Details make sense only when they're presented in a logical framework—an overview of the bottom-line message, followed by elaboration. People will understand the details quicker when you present them in this format, and they'll find your letters, memos, and reports easier to read. To illustrate this format, I've provided two "before" and "after" samples here:

Once-Upon-a-Time Format

Gerri,

So? What does this mean to me?

Revenue brought this to me. Apparently, Blendwold billed us for $154.05 for a joint-venture payout correction on Baytree #1. I had Sandra check on this, and she couldn't find this billing in October or November 19—. Accordingly, Blendwold did not get paid, so they subtracted this amount from the revenue. It took them two checks to do that (see August and September 19— billings).

Oh, I see. My action. Now, how did we get in this mess? Let me start over. . .

Revenue wants us to make an entry to get it off our books. Can you see if this was ever paid? If not, can you have it approved and sent back to me so that I can make an entry? If you have any questions, please call.

MADE Format

Message

Gerri,

Blendwold Company did not get paid for a joint-venture payout correction billing (Baytree #1) dated December 19— for $154.05, so they deducted this bill from our revenue checks. Revenue wants us to make an entry to correct our books.

Action

Would you please check to see if this bill was ever paid? If this bill has not been paid, please have it approved and sent back so that I can make an entry to clear Revenue's books.

Details

I had Sandra check on this, and she could not find where the invoice had been paid in either October or November 19—. Because this bill was a correction, it could have been sent further into 19—. It took Blendwold two checks to make the correction: August 19— and September 19—.

Evidence

I have enclosed copies of the bill and copies of documents showing the expenses subtracted from revenue.

Makes Sense!

Once-Upon-a-Time Format

Subject: Base Program Tape

So?

During the first week of January a system programmer at Albritton Life Insurance tried to install NRWP (program number 5700-XX2) with a tape received June 19—. The base program tape was installed without problems. When the PTF tape was installed, nine prerequisite PTFs seemed to be missing. In a telephone conversation with SID, I was informed that the tape was too old to investigate and that I should order a new copy of NRWP. This new copy was supposed to have solved the problem.

So?

We've got a problem! Now, whose fault is this? Let's start over...

We then were able to continue with the Albritton installation process. There is, however, still a problem with the UPCIN step in the installation. SYP5 has not been updated to reflect the fact that these nine PTFs have already been incorporated into the code. Other clients will incur installation problems similar to ours at Albritton.

I recommend that credit be given to Albritton for the extra installation time required to work through these above problems and for the expedite charge for the new NRWP tape.

MADE Format

Subject: Overcharge to Customer for Defective Installation Tape on NRWP Software

Message

During an installation of the NRWP software program at Albritton Life Insurance, we discovered an error in the installation tape code. Although we billed the customer $980 for the total installation time, approximately half that time was spent investigating and solving our own defective tape code.

Action

Therefore, I recommend that we refund the customer $480 to ensure satisfaction with our program and installation process. This refund represents nine hours' consulting time and $30 for shipping charges on an unnecessary second tape that was supposed to have solved the problem.

I also recommend that the development group immediately send us a temporary solution or set of instructions so that our installers can "work around" the problem until we have a permanent solution.

Details— why

Until our other installers are aware of the problem and temporary solution, we will continue to have customer satisfaction problems involving excessive installation time and the resulting charges.

79

Details— who, how, when

In a phone conversation with Fred Smart of the SID development team on February 4, we were able to verify that the problem is in the UPCIN step of the installation. SYP5 has not been updated to reflect the fact that nine apparently "missing" PTFs have already been incorporated into the base code.

We appreciate Fred Smart's help in determining the problem, but as we both agreed, the solution he gave us was only a temporary one. The NRWP installation code needs to be updated permanently.

Evidence

I've attached the necessary paperwork for you to forward to Accounting if you approve this refund.

Sincerely,

You'll have it made for 90 percent of the messages you communicate—whether on the phone, in person, or in writing—if you use the MADE format as a framework for your ideas and information:

What's the *message?*

What *action* do you want the reader to take? Or, what action do you plan to take?

Here are the *details* ...

I'm enclosing ... (optional *evidence*)

Think MADE. You can avoid reinventing the structure of every document you write, and you can get off the phone quickly.

44. Learn Which Details to Include in Your Formal Correspondence and Reports

People know to be concise, whether they're speaking or writing. That's a given. The issue is, which details to include and which to leave out? The more details we write, the more time it takes to write them and the more time it takes readers to read them.

And what complicates detail selection even further is that we rarely have only one listener or reader. All readers have different levels of knowledge about our subject: Some are technical; some are nontechnical. Some attended a previous meeting; some did not. Some have previous knowledge of the project; some haven't.

They also have different interests in our message. Some want to know about the costs. Some want to know about the safety features. Some want to know about the maintenance agreement. And some are primarily interested in the legal aspects.

So how much detail and how much paperwork do you provide as justification for your decisions and actions?

Here are ten key criteria for deciding how much detail is too much and how little is too little:

1. Who are my readers?
2. What is their bottom-line interest in this information? Why would they want to know what I'm saying?
3. How will they use this information? Will they build on it? Make another decision based on my work?
4. How much do they already know about the subject?
5. Will they be skeptical? If so, what can I do to minimize that skepticism?
6. Will they lose face if they accept my ideas? If so, how can I help them save face?
7. Am I creating extra work for them? If so, how can I make things easier and quicker?
8. Will there be resistance to any change that my message entails? If so, what would push them to act?
9. Is this a low priority? If so, how can I make it sound more urgent?
10. Is this a money issue? Am I asking them to spend more or less than they expected? If so, what will make the investment seem worthwhile?

Asking yourself these questions will prompt you to include the appropriate details. If you don't expect skepticism, then you don't need to elaborate on why. For example, if you're going to tell your boss that you can save over forty thousand dollars next year alone by changing suppliers for a particular piece of equipment, you don't need to elaborate on why *you* need to save forty thousand dollars.

On the other hand, if you're saying you can save forty thousand dollars if you change vendors and you're writing to your boss who chose the current vendor, he or she might be on the defensive about making a bad decision. That tells you you're going to have to elaborate on the proposed change and help the boss save face about what may have been a justifiable decision at an earlier time in a different situation.

The ten questions above will help you eliminate much of the unnecessary length in documents, phone conversations, and meetings, thus saving time for all concerned.

45. "Layer" Your Documents for the Appropriate Audiences

How often do you read every word of every document that comes to you? Neither do most people. Readers read selectively.

So how do you help readers "pick and choose" what they need from your paperwork?

First, identify and rank your readers in order of importance. Consider the decision makers, the readers who must carry out the actions you describe in your document, and those readers who are just reading to be informed.

The most important readers should get their information first. Lower-ranking readers should have to read further into the document to get the information they need. Do not count on the lawyers to read the engineering details of a product. Do not count on the engineers to read the legal aspects and safety issues that governmental agencies will concern themselves with. Don't depend on those dealing with governmental regulations to be concerned with the sales projections.

To each his own—details, that is.

By organizing your document with the big-picture message up front for all readers, followed by the most-important to least-important details set off with informative headings, you can help your readers skim, overview, and review your paperwork quickly and efficiently.

Who knows, maybe they'll follow your model and return the favor, thereby reducing your own reading load.

Overview for all readers

Subject: Corporate Library Study

The Zipher Company library has become nonfunctional; because of overcrowded conditions, fewer and fewer employees are using its services. At an annual cost of $____, the library should serve a vital function in our operations.

Action for decision makers

Office Services recommends that an independent consultant or disinterested employee make a study of how many employees now use the library, or would use it if services were improved. The study should also include suggestions for alleviating the space problem and for improving services.

Details for those who need them

skimming begins here

I've outlined below the areas that need special attention: technical files, parts catalogs, and periodicals.

Technical Files
   (details to follow here...)
Parts Catalogs
   (details to follow here...)
Periodicals
   (details to follow here...)

46. Be Direct When You Write—Use Specific, Clear Words and Short Sentences

"Pursuant to our discussion it seemed imperative that a suitable token of our admiration and esteem should be forthcoming" takes a lot longer to write than "We are sending a gift to show how much we appreciate and admire your work." Likewise with the following:

In the event that	When
At this point in time	Now
We have attempted to discover	We've tried
We will conduct an investigation into	We will investigate
He was found to be in agreement on	He agreed
Significantly unrealized gains	Big losses
Limited resources with which to work	Available funds
Technical exposures that may not go unnoticed among those with which we initiate contractual arrangements	Software errors that customers will notice

When you're indirect and vague in your communications, you'll almost always create extra work for yourself—follow-up memos, phone conversations, and meetings to clarify.

On the other hand, when you're direct and specific, you generally can take care of most situations the first time around.

A side benefit is that when you're direct with others, they generally return the favor. As a result, you'll have to do less "reading between the lines" to decode political messages. In the end, clarity and directness reduce the paperwork shuffle for all concerned.

47. Judge Length by Reading Time and Access, Not Pages

"Put it on a page." That arbitrary rule leads to bad judgment and time-consuming reading.

I applaud brevity, which is what some people mean with the directive "put in on a page."

But there's little correlation between page count and *paperwork time*.

Paper is cheap. Reading-and-writing time is expensive. Some people can cram enormous amounts of information on a page in long paragraphs, with no headings, little white space, slim margins. Their colleagues, on the other hand, tend to spread out information, allow ample white space, use bulleted lists rather than paragraphs, and add informative headings. Bless them.

Such layout techniques (with headings, bullets, lists, and white space) allow readers to skim. These techniques make information accessible.

Which of the two documents below would you read more quickly if you wanted to know when to go to lunch?

(Version 1)

General Operating Policy

A few operating policies that will help orient you to your new position are described below.

You will be asked to prepare an activity report each week. This report will update the current status of training activities as well as any projects on which you are working. It is due by the close of business (COB) each Monday. The collection point for reports is a basket located within the ERC section office.

The standard work week established for Miller International consists of a total of forty hours, staggered by section from 7:30-4:00, 8:00-4:30, or 8:30-5:00. We are open to the public from 8:00-4:30. Although building 5 is available on all shifts, regular hours are from 7:30-4:00.

Lunch duration is thirty minutes, taken at any time between 11:00 and 2:00.

Graysheets are used to record your time. It is important that you complete them daily. You must then transfer this record to your timecard, sign the timecard at the end of each period, and submit it weekly to your section head.

Absences need to be reported to section heads by contacting either the section secretary or the project engineering secretary.

Section meetings are held in the building 5 conference room and are scheduled as needed.

(Version 2)

General Operating Policy

A few operating policies that will help orient you to your new position are described below.

Activity Reports

You will be asked to prepare an activity report each week. This report will update the current status of training activities as well as any projects on which you are working. It is due by the close of business (COB) each Monday. The collection point for reports is a basket located within the ERC section office.

Work Hours

The standard work week established for Miller International consists of a total of forty hours, staggered by section from 7:30-4:00, 8:00-4:30, or 8:30-5:00. We are open to the public from 8:00-4:30. Although building 5 is available on all shifts, regular hours are from 7:30-4:00.

Duration of Lunch

Lunch duration is thirty minutes, taken at any time between 11:00 and 2:00.

Graysheets/Timecards

Graysheets are used to record your time. It is important that you complete them daily. You must then transfer this record to your timecard, sign the timecard at the end of each period, and submit it weekly to your section head.

Reporting Absences

Absences need to be reported to section heads by contacting either the section secretary or the project engineering secretary.

Section Meetings

Section meetings are held in the building 5 conference room and are scheduled as needed.

Do the same for your readers. Don't be hemmed in by the arbitrary "put it on a page" rule for yourself or for others.

When evaluating paperwork, consider reading time, not trees.

48. Forget the Idea that "More Is Better"

How many of your professors gave you assignments by length? "I want a five-hundred-word essay..." or "Your report should be at least ten pages in order to cover the subject." The carryover to that thinking in the business world is: More is better.

More is *not* better. There is no correlation between quantity and quality. Don't get trapped thinking, "The more money I want customers to spend, the more detail I should give them to justify the price." Or, "The more serious this problem, the more detail I should give to support my solution and to impress upon the reader the urgency of making a quick decision."

The Declaration of Independence has fewer than 1,400 words. The most often quoted speech, the Gettysburg Address, has only 272 words. The Sermon on the Mount has only 2,381 words. Consider the importance of what you have to say and tailor your comments accordingly.

More is *not* better. Less means more—more readers, more insight, more impact, more attention.

49. Practice Completed Staff Work

Many times we have to redo our paperwork because of insufficient understanding of what constitutes completed staff work. Here's the major difference between the thinking of senior executives and support staff people:

The support staff person says, "I wasn't asked to give a recommendation; I was simply asked a question. My document, therefore, should provide information to answer the question."

The senior executive reasons, "I asked a question; I want not just an answer, but also a recommendation for the next step." That's completed staff work.

To reduce your paperwork on any given situation, think like the senior executive—completed staff work.

For example, someone says to you, "Registrants are complaining about Orlando for the convention. Do you think we can find suitable accommodations if we change the site on such short notice?" Don't respond with a memo or letter saying simply yes or no and providing reasons for your answer. If you do, the other person will then have to generate correspondence back to you to ask for recommendations on a new site and to ask you to "look into" the details of the site change.

Don't wait for others to take you to the next step. Think ahead as you prepare your paperwork. Rather than just answer questions or describe problems, make recommendations to take the situation to the next stage.

All that should be left for a boss to do where you're concerned is to sign the attached paperwork approving your recommendation.

What's the flipside? Three or four interactions between you and the boss on any given situation. More paperwork and delayed action.

Aim to complete the job on the first go-around.

50. Determine a Hierarchy of Values for Editing and Rewriting

Are you one of those individuals who always feel they need to tweak the final draft just one more time to "get it just right"?

Our research shows that the average document is rewritten 4.5 times—before it even gets to the intended reader! Now that's a productivity problem!

Yes, you can almost always improve your work. I don't know a professional writer who doesn't see a final book manuscript before it goes to press and have the urge to change some word, phrase, or idea. But consider the point of diminishing returns on time invested—especially in the corporate world.

Consider the following guidelines for editorial changes:

• **Content:** Are the facts correct? Is the information complete? Is the message, recommendation, and any follow-up action clear and up front? Appropriate or rambling details? Too much or too little explanation?

• **Layout:** Does the document have informative headings and adequate white space so that readers can skim to preview and review? Does the document make good use of the list format for easy reading and recall of key points?

- **Clarity:** Are there unclear, ambiguous words, phrases, or sentences? Unsupported opinions? Broad generalizations with little impact?

- **Grammar:** Poor grammar affects both clarity and image. Yes, do correct subjects and verbs that don't agree and dangling phrases that don't make sense. But should you really rewrite a document simply to add the serial comma when both ways of punctuating are correct?

- **Style:** Should you say "happy" or "glad"? Should you say, "We recommend" or "Huffco International recommends"? Always question the time and expense required to rewrite documents for such style reasons.

Keep in mind the point of diminishing returns in editing your own work. As in negotiations, set a "walk-away" price.

51. Stifle the Urge to Edit Others' Writing

Someone has said, "The world's strongest drive is not love or hate. It is one person's need to change another's copy." Are you one of those managers who feel they haven't done their job if they haven't edited a document sent to them for approval?

If so, think again. Your continual rewriting of others' work limits their own improvement. For the most part, you're creating frustration and a "Why bother?" attitude. They will take less and less responsibility for their own work and continue to send you worse and worse copy. You'll find yourself editing/rewriting more and more, and they'll learn less and less.

When you're in a position to edit others' work, don't do their job for them. Instead, teach the writers what you're doing. Most frustrated writers complain that they receive no feedback about why a document was accepted in one case and rejected in another case.

As you review, pencil notes in the margin such as, "This sounds too directive for the situation, don't you think?" Or, "Need some informative headings in this section." Or, "Is this detailed explanation really necessary?" Or, "Please expand this section to include our marketing plans."

In other words, make comments and raise questions, and then return the document to colleagues or subordinates for a rewrite. You'll improve their writing and give them ownership.

And you'll eventually save yourself enormous amounts of time on future paperwork sent for your review.

52. Get Off Others' Distribution Lists

"But isn't information power?" you may be asking. Yes, information is power. And yes, you want to know what's going on. But don't equate information and power with *paper*. Information doesn't have to come in hard copy. Twenty pages long. Single-spaced. Instead, pick up the telephone, attend a meeting, or walk around in the hallway. Let someone else wade through the written details—someone who's not as interested in being productive.

So what's the harm with a copy here and a copy there? You have to read things to find out you didn't need to read them after all. What's more, copies often demand a response. Is the writer wanting an answer, a go-ahead, a thank-you, a follow-up phone call? Will you be considered delinquent if you don't generate paperwork in response?

When you get a copy of something you don't need, let the sender know. Return the document with a note saying you no longer have use for this or that report. You don't have to be blunt; just jot a "thanks, but no thanks" comment about why you no longer need the information contained in the report or memo. Attach the buck slip to the report, and return it to the sender, asking him or her to remove your name from that distribution list permanently.

Don't get bogged down in reading everybody else's junk mail at work any more than you read the junk mail at home addressed to "Dear Occupant."

53. Update Your Distribution Lists and Consider the "Need to Know"

For years, career counselors advised people on how to play politics within the organization. Part of that political game was linked to networking, and specifically networking via the internal communication channels. Seeing your name on a distribution list, along with others at the executive level, was equated with being invited to play on the high school all-star team. Likewise, having your name omitted was tantamount to being "uninvited" to the senior prom.

Some colleagues learned those networking skills all too well. They began to copy everybody on everything—just to cover themselves in case someone "should have" received information that they generated. Within short order, people became inundated with irrelevant information—information that they didn't know they didn't want or need until they'd already expended the time and effort to read it.

Now, corporate colleagues are crying uncle. Their electronic mail and their in-baskets overfloweth! They can't possibly read all that comes to them, and they discard much of what's sent without so much as a glance. Often they're angry to have been duped into reading what they erroneously assumed was important.

Sending copies of everything to everybody will make you, the guilty writer, appear not to understand what's important and what's not. Just because it takes *you* very little effort to touch a key and send a copy to the world, consider the poor readers on the other end who must sort through the deluge.

54. Send Things Only When People Ask for Them

When you no longer have an inclination to prepare a certain document, don't—unless you hear sharp, prolonged objections. And don't recant just because you hear a whimper or two. Consider this paraphrase of an old axiom: What they don't know won't hurt them—but what they expect and no longer receive may cause a mild whine.

Although you may have shaped others' expectations by your previous efforts, they may not necessarily *need* your paperwork to get their job done. Rather than create expectations, let others decide what they need from you; then consider complying.

If you can't determine who should get copies, attach a note to your document: "This report is compiled monthly from information received in our XYZ department. If you still need this information from us, would you please let us know by signing and returning the attached form."

So what if no one returns the form? Assume that no one read your note or your report. Remove their names from your distribution list. If you still don't hear any objections, smile. One less report to write each month.

55. Help People Route What You Send Them

Add a routing slip to the cover of reports, professional journals, or article excerpts you want others to see. When individuals finish reading the document you've routed to them, have them line through their names and send the document on to the next person on the list.

In addition to eliminating the growing mound of paperwork waiting to be read in "leisure time," this routing lowers subscription costs, reduces storage and maintenance costs, and encourages sharing of ideas/reactions penciled in the margins—ideas that might never be exchanged if everyone had his or her own copy.

Knowing that someone else is waiting to read the circulated information also forces people to make an immediate decision—either they need/want to know the information or they don't. Players read or pass.

56. Post Information of General Interest

Don't limit your thinking about bulletin board use to include only job openings, fire drill regulations, announcements of the upcoming blood drive, and photos from the annual company picnic.

Make bulletin boards useful *and* a common area for networking. If you make an effort to keep boards up-to-date, people will learn to count on them for vital information.

And you don't have to have a formal bulletin board to use this idea. Post information *anywhere people pass or gather*. Consider the restroom walls as a prime place.

Having information at walking eye level is preferable to having it at the bottom of the pile on everyone's desk.

57. Write and Post Instructions to Operate Equipment Once and for All

Wherever there's a machine, there's a person who doesn't know how to operate it. And it's often easier for that bewildered person to ask someone for help than to learn how to operate the equipment through trial and error. That is, it's easier *if you're the bewildered person*. But if you're the person who's always being interrupted by every passerby who needs instructions . . .

Even if you're not in the general line for questions about the copier, switchboard, video player, or whatever, why should your kids phone you at work to find out how to operate the clothes dryer?

For any equipment at home or business, write step-by-step instructions in plain English. Then hand the instructions to a guinea pig or two and watch while they operate the equipment with your instructions. If the operator has difficulty or asks for clarification, modify your instructions until they are clear.

Then, when others ask you for help, refer them to the already prepared instructions, emphasizing that those written directions will probably be clearer and more thorough than your off-the-cuff attempt.

One preparation for all help requests—that's your goal.

58. Write and Duplicate Fliers Containing Answers to Frequently Asked Questions

Prospective customers ask about prices and benefits. Contributors to fund-raisers ask how the money will be spent. Renters ask their landlords about contracts, payments, due dates, and late charges. Whatever the situation or event, people tend to ask the same questions over and over.

Regardless of your job or project, once you've been at it long enough, you'll identify the recurring questions and issues. To reduce your paperwork in writing long, complex individual responses to each inquirer, record your answers beforehand in fliers, brochures, or simple one-page letters.

In other words, broaden your thinking about the terms *brochure* and *flier*: I'm not talking about a twenty-thousand-dollar product/service brochure; I'm relating the information-distribution concept to everyday situations—those every bit as time-consuming as the sales call. And in those situations, a one-page, double-spaced, attractively laid-out "answer sheet" is a handy solution.

The topic may be answers to any of the following: "What's the money going to be used for?" "Who's eligible for that benefit?" "How do I submit a suggestion?" "What will take this spot out of my clothes?" "What kind of information do I need to provide for you to cash my check?" "What's the CD rate this week?" "What committees does this organization have that I might be interested in serving on, and what does each committee do?"

Then the next time a caller begins to ask similar questions, offer to send the flier "so that your information will be complete and thorough." Even when the individual visits you face-to-face to ask these routine questions, you can always provide these fliers as a "take-away" piece for later reference.

Having such information available to send at a moment's notice reduces the number of original responses you'll need to draft. Fewer answers mean more time for the real project.

59. Develop Personalized Model Letters

Never write a letter in vain. Our research shows that the average writer takes approximately sixty-five minutes to compose a one-page letter. Increase the return on your investment by saving every letter that you can reuse.

However, a letter saved is no good unless you can retrieve it. Don't trust your memory. "Didn't I write a letter about this very same thing last spring? Or was it last fall? To a Mr. Brown. Or was it Brunson? Or something like that."

Filing reusable letters by meaningless names or dates makes them next to impossible to find. Rather, keep a model-letter binder and file your reusable correspondence by subject and variation of detail. For example, here are a few tabs we use in our office for filing model letters:

Inquiry—writing workshop only
Inquiry—writing workshop and oral presentations
Inquiry—writing, oral presentations, customer-service
     communications
Inquiry—oral presentation only
Inquiry—customer-service communications only
Inquiry—train-the-trainer course only
Inquiry—books
Inquiry—videos
Inquiry—audios
Inquiry—writing workshops and books
Inquiry—keynote speeches
Inquiry—consulting services
Inquiry—editorial services
Thank you for buying books
Thank you for booking speech

Thank you for booking workshop
Thank you for referral
Thank you for reviewing our book
Thank you for guest appearance on radio/TV
Declining to do business—not our field
Declining to do business—conflict of interest
Declining to do business—time frame
Declining to do business—unprofitable for us
Confirmation of scheduling workshop
Confirmation of scheduling speech
Confirmation of TV/radio appearance

We have more, but you get the idea.

Having boilerplate models *does not* mean, however, that you will use them verbatim. That's the biggest mistake you can make as a salesperson—to send boilerplate letters to prospects and customers, letters that do not meet their real needs or answer their specific questions.

You want to use the models simply as models. The wording long developed and tested serves up the basic ideas, but you'll always need to customize the boilerplate with additional sentences or phrases that address the individual reader's needs and situation.

A letter well written should be a letter retrievable and reusable.

60. Use Form Memos for Internal Audiences

Many people shoot themselves in the proverbial foot by sending boilerplate, uncustomized form letters to their customers and then writing originally worded documents to internal audiences. Wrong approach. Spend time where it really counts: Write personalized letters to customers and use shortcuts for internal readers.

Whatever situation you find yourself repeatedly responding to, develop standardized responses so that all your reader has to do is check a box or write in a word and send the information on its way to you.

There's no need to reinvent the structure when you respond to the same issues internally:

- "Where are the receipts for the travel expense report you submitted? We need to have those on file before we can issue your reimbursement check."
- "The attached memo does not have the appropriate approval signatures. Please have those individuals sign, and then please resubmit your report."
- "Your address change has been processed. If you do not receive your mail at the new

address within five days, please notify us again at extension 123."

Analyze what most of your paperwork is about and spend a few hours developing boilerplate responses. Or develop them as you go.

If you already have on hand such form responses or notices but they still generate questions from your colleagues, rework the boilerplates. Get out the bugs and keep the system humming without additional phone calls or paperwork.

61. Understand the Real Cost of Processing Forms

Once you get the cost estimate from the printer or in-house graphics department about how much a form will cost, stop and think. This form will cost you about forty times that amount for distributing, processing, storing, and retrieving the information gathered. It's not the cost of paper and printing that's the culprit; it's the cost of completing the forms and processing them that causes nightmares.

Yes, forms are useful (1) when they save you

time by eliminating the need to compose an original letter or memo to collect certain information, and (2) when they save someone else's time in drafting a response.

But before you design a new form, ask:

- Is this same information already available somewhere else?
- Could I use an existing form to extract the same information?
- Could I modify an existing form to add one or two items, thus eliminating the need for this new form?
- Is the form self-explanatory, or will I need to add a cover letter/memo "to explain"?
- Is the form confusing?

Understand the time required in interpreting a form, completing it, transferring the information to a usable state (such as computer entry), processing the information, and retrieving the information. Is the information worth the cost? Are you sure?

62. Use Well-Designed Forms

After my divorce, I wrote a credit card company to ask them to change the status of a jointly held account to my name only. I included the full names on the current account, gave the date of divorce, stated that I would assume full responsibility for the balance of the account, enclosed the appropriate income information, along with my ex-spouse's cut-up card.

I got a form letter from the credit card company with a check mark beside form statement 2: "Please return the cut-up card of the cardholder to be dropped from the account."

I wrote a second time to explain that I had enclosed the cut-up card the first time.

Again, I got a form letter from the credit card company, with a check mark beside form statement 4: "Please have both cardholders' signatures notarized." I had already done that on the first letter.

I wrote for the third time, explaining that both requirements had been met with the first correspondence.

Finally, I got a form letter from the credit card company with a check mark beside the statement: "The actions you've requested with regard to your account have been taken."

Evidently, their own forms were inadequate to explain exactly what I hadn't done correctly to get the account changed, and I—or they—accidentally got things right the third time around.

Forms and form letters can be exasperating to customers, not to mention time-consuming and expensive when they're confusing and inappropriate for the situation or information they're supposed to gather.

Before you infuriate someone and waste your time and theirs on paperwork, keep these guidelines in mind for good form design.

- Give the form a title that clearly signals its purpose.
- Give the form a number for better control and reference.
- Consider the weight and grade of paper to make sure the form is suitable for the intended handling. Will all copies be readable?
- Include instructions with (or on) the form itself.
- Tell where the form came from and where the respondent is supposed to send it.
- Put the key data in the easiest-to-read spots.
- Place the items in the same order as they will need to be entered on other forms or into the computer.
- Break information into logical sections.
- Use color or shading to separate sections.
- Use color coding for copies to be routed to different places.

- Leave adequate space to enter the requested information—whether entered on typewriter, computer, or by hand.
- Leave adequate space for all signatures.
- Use complete terms. Don't say "quarter." Do you mean "reporting quarter" or "sales quarter"? Don't say "time." Do you mean "time of accident" or "time of notification to company"?
- Use the same terms for the same items on the form. Don't call something a "warehouse" and then later refer to the same thing as a "storage site."
- Try to avoid open-ended questions. Instead, print answer choices with check boxes. Put the boxes to be checked *before* the items rather than after.
- Use simple words and short sentences with the item titles and explanations. Don't say "Where did you obtain the equipment?" when you can say "Where did you get the projector?" Don't say "This percentage rate will accrue to your account" when you can say "This interest will be added to your account."
- Give instructions about where and how to include additional, unusual explanations about various items.
- Give a department, position title, or phone number to contact for questions about the form.

Don't decide to design forms by chance. Inappropriately designed forms cost time and money and cause headaches.

63. Use Personal, Applicable Letters to Customers

No, this tip doesn't contradict the previous advice to retain and reuse boilerplate letters. Rather, this tip goes a step further: In the current lean-and-mean business environment, a personal letter packs punch and power. Why? Because (1) most people hate to write, and (2) they have no spare time. For the routine, they feel more comfortable and productive in picking up the phone.

Writing a special letter says to the customer that you care enough to put extra effort into the contact.

When you get rid of the unnecessary paperwork on your desk, the really important letters that need to be written get your priority time and energy. The dividends of that special letter at the right time can be enormous.

64. Talk Rather than Write to Give Mild Reprimands

When *how* you say something is as important as *what* you say, talk the message. You'll save time and a possible negative reaction that will necessitate a second written response.

Written reprimands have other drawbacks. For one, they take away the reader's dignity. After all, somebody has to type the reprimand, somebody else may open and read the mail, and then somebody has to file it. Each pair of eyes adds to the receiver's embarrassment.

A second problem is the recovery rate. With spoken words, the listener tends to focus on the content—the problem and the corrective action. With the written reprimand, the reader tends to lick his or her wounds longer and even dream of retorts and retaliations. You as writer often want to temper the words so that they spur corrective action and mean no more and no less than you intend. But black-and-white words on a page sound cold, stern, ominous. They lack a supportive smile and an understanding nod or pat on the back.

Aware of all these possible reactions, you as writer aim to get the tone "just right." Therefore, you tend to write and rewrite, write and rewrite.

Unless the situation will have later legal repercussions, talk a mild reprimand. Writing a reprimand means time—time spent crafting the exact wording with a precise tone.

65. Talk Rather than Write to Send Trial Balloons

Skilled politicians have perfected the art of floating trial balloons. The technique can be equally useful to you.

When you want to see how an idea plays in Peoria before committing it to policy or procedure, talk that idea to your colleagues and even to your customers. Sending up a trial balloon does not mean, however, that you should word the idea carelessly, with little thought to the phrasing and the detailed explanation and support. Plan the spoken balloon just as you would a written one. Then "casually" mention your thinking in a staff meeting, in the hallway by the water cooler, or at lunch with a customer.

In fact, you can even float the communication as a "rumor" you heard from someone else. Check the reaction, hear the questions raised, anticipate and plan how you'll handle the complaints.

If the idea turns out to be a bad one, you've saved yourself the trouble of writing it into policy or procedure form.

If the idea flies, the talking trial balloon has focused attention and garnered reactions that will result in a better policy, procedure, or decision once committed to writing.

66. Talk Rather than Write to Persuade the Uninterested

Telemarketers have learned this principle the hard way. Marketing is much more effective when a salesperson makes contact first by telephone, then follows up with the written message. In a written message, you can lose a reader in the blink of an eye; while face-to-face, or even on the telephone, you have a slightly longer opportunity to arouse interest.

That's why employment counselors suggest that job applicants do almost anything to talk to a prospective employer rather than just drop a résumé in the mail. They have a much better chance of getting their voice "in the door" than a piece of paper.

The same is true in most other situations. Consider fund-raising. Which strategy gets the best results: the direct-mail appeal, the telephone call, or the personal appointment?

When you need to sell a boss on an idea, talk first. A piece of paper is much easier to toss aside than a body. Then when you get as far as a fair hearing, switch tactics to paper to prove that you have thoroughly evaluated your idea or recommendation.

Talk to get attention. Then write to add the "meat" and prove you know what you're talking about.

67. Talk Rather than Write to Negotiate Small Details

Why write when half of what you say will have to be changed in later negotiations?

I've spent months in contract negotiations simply because both parties insisted on putting their offers in writing rather than talking. Shuffling paragraphs that have been added, amended, qualified, and initialed certainly takes more time than talking through the give-and-take and then drafting the written document. (Yes, I'm aware of the negotiating tactic to be the first to put something in writing. The hope there is to intimidate the other party by implying that further changes will jeopardize the deal.)

But don't limit your thinking simply to formal contracts. Our everyday business operations require us to negotiate all sorts of things:

Which projects am I to follow up on? And which will you handle?

What's the real due date on this and what penalties are involved if I miss the deadline?

If we rent the ballroom for the cocktail hour, how much will you knock off the luncheon price per person?

In any of these situations, talk is by far the cheapest and quickest method of negotiating situations and details. Nail down the whens, whys, and wherefores; *then* write to confirm, *if necessary*. (See tip 20 before you confirm.)

68. Talk Rather than Write to Get Immediate Feedback

Why delay your own work, when you can pick up the phone or walk down the hall to talk to a person in real time?

Waiting itself creates paperwork. Why? Because most of us can't wait in silence. We send follow-up reminders beginning, "I was talking with Joe Smoe last week about the XYZ project and that reminded me that I still had not heard from you about..." And then the typical response arrives: "I have delayed in writing you about the XYZ project because we are still waiting on a decision about..." More paperwork. Still no answers.

Waiting builds frustration. The bigger the organization or the department, the longer the usual wait for an answer. Take the initiative in deciding what can wait for a written answer and what you should take care of immediately. Trust your judgment about adverse effects of delay; and eventually, if you're right most of the time, the boss or your colleagues will come to trust your need-to-know-now interruptions without the red tape.

69. Talk Rather than Write When You Need to See a Reaction to Your Message

An even bigger benefit of talk is seeing the physical reaction of another person to your message. "Joanna, we're going to be transferring you to Anchorage" may bring a written letter accepting the transfer but hide a negative reaction that would tell you Joanna doesn't plan to be with you much longer.

Delivering the Anchorage message on the phone or face-to-face gives you immediate insight to the other's reaction. The disappointed tone of voice or the apprehensive stare conveys much more than a written letter of compliance would ever reveal.

Saving time on the paperwork is a bonus.

70. Talk Rather than Write When "How You Say It" Is as Important as "What You Say"

Written words fall flat. They often fail to convey the drama or import of a situation. Studies show that only 7 percent of our message comes from the actual words we use. Ninety-three percent of our impact comes from our tone, voice quality, and physical appearance.

Consequently, many people who have first been persuaded with talk become dissuaded when they read the whole situation in black print on white paper. Customers particularly hesitate when they get to the paperwork or "fine print" part of buying. That is, they like to own, not to buy—they often balk at signing the "official" paperwork.

Additionally, bad news doesn't seem quite so bad when spoken in an optimistic, upbeat tone. Support, commitment to a project or a person, and willingness to compromise can best be conveyed through inflection, a lifted eyebrow, an upturned mouth, or a nod of the head. Paper conveys only one-dimensional words.

Why put extra time into writing when the spoken word can better convey a caring tone?

71. Take Talk Seriously

In our culture, we have "inherited" the idea that important or "official" things come only in written form—such as drivers' licenses, tax appraisals, birth certificates, death certificates, divorce decrees. But "official" doesn't necessarily mean "written." Talk can be official, too. If the CEO asks you to stop by his or her office before you leave for the day, that's official—whether it's spoken in the cafeteria, phoned in by the secretary, or written on presidential letterhead.

Doesn't everybody take talk seriously? Of course not. A marketing representative shared this situation with me: He had repeatedly tried to get his manager's attention about a lack of proper inventory controls and constant delays in processing orders on the correct shipping dates. He had discussed the problem with the manager on the phone, he had left a message for him on his electronic message system, and he had also mentioned the problem in a staff meeting. But his boss had given him no response whatsoever. After expressing his frustration to me, the marketing rep finally sighed, "I guess what I'm going to have to do is to put it in a formal letter to him. That's the only way anybody ever gets his attention."

Why create extra reading for yourself by ignoring talk?

72. Use an Assistant to Prewrite

Does this sound like the typical incoming mail/outgoing response routine?

Assistant opens the mail and lays the incoming letter on the boss's desk.

Boss reads the letter mentioning an upcoming convention and inviting her to meet for dinner on Tuesday night of the convention. Boss wonders if her schedule will allow her to attend the convention at all. She pencils note to the assistant in the margin of the letter: "Would you check on the dates for the strategic planning meeting in June? I think I may have a conflict with this convention date."

Assistant verifies that the dates do conflict and jots that note on the letter, returning it to the boss's desk.

Boss reads that note and asks the assistant to draft a reply to the colleague, declining the invitation for dinner.

The assistant drafts a reply and puts it on the boss's desk.

The boss reads the assistant's draft, makes a few editorial changes, and returns it to the assistant's desk for a rewrite.

The assistant rewrites the letter and returns it to the boss for a signature.

Boss signs and returns the letter to the assistant to mail.

That document has changed hands eight times before it ever hits the outgoing mail.

That's inefficiency. An assistant should be able to draft routine replies and attach them to incoming mail before that mail goes on the boss's desk for review. All that the boss should have to do is read the incoming correspondence and sign the outgoing response. And that routine should be the rule, not the exception.

Keeping a binder of model documents to be customized and personalized (as mentioned in tip 59) will be an invaluable resource for your assistant in such drafting. And, of course, unusual circumstances may alter the routine for further instructions or explanations about unusual responses.

What else should your assistant be able to do to reduce your paperwork? Plenty. She should be able to collect information that you'll need to review before drafting a lengthy report. Your assistant should be able to organize and sort that information into a usable form. She should be able to take a rough draft you've completed on the computer and "pretty it up" by breaking long paragraphs and combining choppy ones, by turning long complex blocks into bulleted lists, and by adding informative headings. Additionally, the assistant should be able to proofread and correct clarity problems or grammatical errors.

If your assistant does not now do these tasks, why not? Many well-educated assistants are more than willing and able to take on these additional tasks. If yours is unwilling or incapable of such paperwork, teach her to write effectively, send her to a writing course, or find a replacement who has mastered these skills. Then learn to delegate writing and prewriting tasks more efficiently (see earlier tips 10, 13, 14, 36, 43, 49).

Make paperwork the forte of your administrative assistant.

73. Use an Assistant to Preread

A *good* assistant opens the morning mail. A *great* assistant reads it. Then she gathers and attaches all applicable documents for the boss's reply or drafts the reply herself. (See the previous tip.)

But mail duty doesn't stop with correspondence. An assistant should preread reports, highlighting key facts and ideas of interest. She should preview the tables of contents of magazines and journals to highlight articles of interest. She also should read and highlight key ideas in these articles—articles that you may miss in your own hurried skimming.

Of course, this prereading task assumes that you will keep your assistant thoroughly informed about your current and future plans and projects so that she'll know of your reading interests. Certain things always require highlighting: advertisements by competitors, key industry news, dates for major events, and so forth.

Your assistant also should read all incoming requests and jot explanations to you in the margin. For example, if someone returns one of your reports with a note asking for an explanation about why the projected expenses were so far off for April, she should have looked up that information and reminded you in the margin: "The April figures were high because we prepaid the printing costs." Or some such.

Even the junk mail, which you don't have time to read in detail, if at all, can be a source of valuable information. Instruct your assistant to preread it, to discard what she knows is of no interest, and to route anything to you that may have educational value—an advertisement for new equipment, a seminar topic directed to your interest, a startling industry happening.

With a little give-and-take, you and your assistant can form a team that shifts most of the paperwork from your desk to hers—a team that concentrates on the important and discards the time wasters.

74. Establish Priorities

All paperwork tasks are not created equal. The 80-20 rule applies here: 80 percent of the results come from 20 percent of the paperwork.

Many efficient people take great pains to plan all the events of the day, week, or month according to priority. And then they lump all the paperwork projects into one four-hour block on a Friday afternoon and play paperwork pileup.

Paperwork—if it's important enough to be done at all—deserves a priority scheduling just like any other task. If the paperwork is so routine that it can easily be lumped into "paperwork," reexamine your thinking to see if the tasks are necessary at all. Assign low payoff tasks to your assistant or simply stop doing them. If the paperwork actually brings results, then schedule the task right along with other priority events.

Constantly fight the battle of plateauing paperwork. If any particular paperwork doesn't pay off for you or the company over time, question it. Question your customers about it. (Do they really want you to bill them for the extra time the paperwork costs?) Question your boss about it. (Does the boss really want a written trip report when you can give him your observations in thirty seconds?)

Become a broken record if need be:

"Now exactly why did you say I needed to recompile these figures from the district report into the regional report?"

"Why is it exactly that MIS can't merge these reports for us?"

"Why is X necessary when we discussed all the key issues in staff meeting last week? Okay, but this report will require about six hours of my time that I sure could put to use elsewhere."

Such reminders and questioning will make a boss think twice, or three times, about continuing to tie you up with paperwork.

And when you set your own priorities, remind yourself that paperwork should gain a priority standing equivalent to the results it generates.

75. Psych Yourself out of Procrastination

Paperwork piles up in direct proportion to your penchant for procrastination. Show me a pile of paperwork that has accumulated over a period of weeks or months, and I'll show you someone who avoids decisions.

Here's how indecision creates the paperwork pileup: You pick up a piece of paper, can't decide whether to start on the project or to wait for more information before making a decision, and return the paperwork to the pile for "later." Tomorrow you pick up the same piece of paper, reread it, rethink the situation, and return it to the pile. Next week, you're sorting through the pile for something else and find the paper again. Now, what was this all about? You reread it. Still not ready to commit to a decision, you return the paper to the pile once again. Read it. Move it. Forget it. Read it. Move it. Forget it. There's a sense of activity, but no gain.

Consider these tricks to psych yourself out of procrastinating with paperwork:

- Reward yourself with ten minutes of "recess" (longer lunch, afternoon break, Friday afternoon golf) for every piece of paper you handle.
- Reward yourself with a dollar bill (or five dollars) dropped into a box for an indulgent only-me splurge for every piece of paper you handle. With the money, go shopping on the way home.
- Break the formidable task into small chunks. You can do one step of anything. Make the phone calls to request the necessary

information that goes into the report. Or, outline the key ideas. Or, locate the drawing you plan to attach as an appendix. Do one little thing.

- Tell other people about your procrastination habit and commit to them your plans to catch up by a certain date. You'll be embarrassed to tell them that you've still done nothing.
- Visualize a clean desk and a stress-free weekend with no paperwork pileup to face on Monday morning.
- Visualize the negative consequences of losing your job if you don't set priorities for the paperwork and get it done.
- Talk to yourself differently. Instead of dreading the paperwork and haranguing yourself, your boss, your customers, and your family about doing it, calculate the individual pieces of paperwork as milestones to your goal. Just as sales reps know their averages on phone calls (for example, that it takes eighteen calls to make a sale), know your average with paperwork. How many pieces of paper do you have to handle to complete a sale? And if you're not a salesperson, consider your annual salary and divide it by the pieces of paper you handle in a year. For every piece of paper handled then, you can consider that paper as being twelve dollars toward your salary. When you stop handling the paper, the salary may stop.

Whatever method you choose, psych yourself out of procrastinating—a habit that only compounds the paperwork pile.

76. Use Prime Time on Payoff Paper

The typical way to tackle paperwork is to start with the easy, no-brain stuff and work your way to the more difficult. Then by the time you get to the tasks that require the most thought, you're already tired and half your allotted time has slipped away. The result? You do less than your best work on the most important tasks or decide not to do the most difficult task at all because you "don't have enough time to finish." Procrastination wins again.

You can see how that habit, allowed to continue, means that you dabble with a little paperwork all along, but the tasks you choose to do are the piddling things that amount to nothing. Important projects, like the major report or the client proposal, go undone.

Reverse that approach. Complete the most important paperwork first during prime time while your energy is high.

Then as energy and time dwindle, you can postpone the less important paperwork without such a negative consequence. Often, after you've completed the most important and most complex paperwork, you're so pleased with yourself that you work right through the less important chores.

If you're on a roll, keep pushing the paper until it's gone.

77. Do the Necessary Paperwork When Nobody Else Is

"The devil made me do it." Those of us who routinely procrastinate like to blame other people. With paperwork, the line goes something like this:

"I was trying to write out the checks this afternoon, but with it raining outside and three kids underfoot..."

"I thought I'd get something done on that Beasley report, but I've had three or four people drop by to chat every time I just about got ready to start it."

"I took that paperwork with me on the plane yesterday and thought I'd get to it. But I had to put my briefcase three rows ahead of me, and I forgot to take out the files before I sat down and buckled up."

Do you recall ever using similar lines? Recognize procrastination for what it is and deal with it (see tip 75 on procrastination).

If, however, you don't diagnose the problem as procrastination in disguise, then the solution may be as simple as swimming upstream. That is, study the schedule of your colleagues around the office or that of your family around the house. If they come in to the office late, arrive early yourself and enjoy the uninterrupted work time. If they come in early, stay late. If they all go out to lunch on Fridays, have lunch at your desk that day and finish the week's paperwork.

Remember that doors are for closing on occasion. Voice mail and/or secretaries are for screening. If you don't have voice mail, an assistant, or doors, you and a colleague can run interference for each other. He answers all your calls and intercepts visitors for you on Thursday mornings, and you do the same for him on Thursday afternoons.

Make it easy on yourself to concentrate. Avoid the temptation to let yourself be interrupted. Look for times and places to work where others aren't.

78. Keep Others Informed So They Can Shoulder the Load

To be the only one who knows when Vendor A will give a volume discount and the only one who knows where Supplier B wants the bid request sent may make you look knowledgeable. But it also increases your responsibility for extra paperwork.

Are you frequently the target of statements like these?

"Do you have the name of those two video-dupe companies we used last year? If so, would you send me those names, numbers, and addresses?"

"Do you have that article that came out in *Training* magazine last month—the one about the quality and productivity links? Would you mind copying that for me and maybe sending Bill Lupus a copy also?"

"Since you're the only one who has been to all the meetings and knows where we've come from on this project, why don't you write up a brief overview to distribute to the whole membership?"

If you're the only one who has the names, numbers, addresses, articles, or background knowledge, you'll feel selfish and rude not to oblige with the information. So, don't be caught as "the only one."

Keep others informed—an assistant, a colleague,

a subordinate, a boss. Leave a trail. When someone begins, "Do you happen to have...," you can respond with, "Yes, that's in the file under 'Blakestone Guest List.' Help yourself, or why don't you call Mary or Ted if you have any other questions. They both have worked right along beside me on that project."

Every little piece of paper handled for someone else means less time for handling your own paperwork. Unless you're bidding on a big contract, don't aim to be the sole-source provider.

79. Do Your Work by Phone When You're out of the Office

The worst part of family vacation is coming home to find a lawn in need of mowing, a laundry bag full of two weeks' playclothes, and a pile of unpaid bills. The equivalent of that scene in the office is the pile of paperwork on your desk—forty-two pink phone messages, six journals, fourteen reports, twenty-eight memos, and six forms that require your data and signature.

After an absence from the office, a pile of

paperwork is *not* inevitable. With phone, fax, and overnight mail, you can keep up with most routine things while away. The trick is to use your travel downtime wisely. For example, you finish a meeting at 5:00 and a cocktail hour is scheduled for 6:00. Call the office and ask your secretary to read your mail to you, dictate your reply, and let her sign it and send the information on its way. Or, say you find out that Thursday evening's convention dinner has been canceled. So have your office overnight you the four reports that you need to review. Maybe that's not as exciting as the former dinner plans, but at least you can get something productive done rather than stewing in your room over a boring evening in front of the TV.

And never go on the road without overnight envelopes, Dictaphone and tapes, and paper paraphernalia.

Even when the absence from the office is due to illness, often you may feel up to a little work by phone just to break the monotony of recuperating. Just fifteen minutes twice a day on the phone with your office can be time enough to work through the day's mail and have phone messages returned on your behalf.

Not only will *you* feel so much better about staying current, but so will those who are waiting for your answers, approvals, or other information. You'd be surprised how informal people will let you be while you're officially "out of the office." When you return those phone calls from colleagues who have requested this or that, begin your comments with something like, "Got your phone message when I called my office at noon. I can give you those numbers on the phone now, or I'll put them in a letter next week when I get back. Which do you prefer—now or later?" More often than not, the person will prefer "now."

And if that doesn't work, be more assertive: "I have that information with me. I'll just give you those numbers now so that you don't have to wait until next week. The first figure is..." One less report to write.

To motivate yourself to call in to the office while away, visualize that paperwork pile that won't be there when you return.

80. Use Travel Time for Paperwork

Travel time represents enormous amounts of downtime if you don't plan ahead. The *Wall Street Journal* recently reported that the average business professional now spends forty days a year "on the road." If you travel, paperwork can ease the pain of missed connections, extended layovers, lonely hotel rooms, and long waiting lines.

First, carry the supplies you need to be efficient. Either in your car, in your luggage, or in your briefcase, carry with you at all times the following: paperclips, stapler, staple remover, pens/pencils, rubber bands, stamps, postcards, letterhead and envelopes, file folders, overnight envelopes, and Dictaphone and tapes or laptop computer.

Second, stay at hotels that cater to business travelers and have secretarial services. The availability of a copy machine, fax, or typing services is worth any extra cost.

Third, carry the *appropriate* paperwork. The easiest work to do while traveling is reading journals, articles, and reports. The next easiest paperwork task on the road is to compose short documents. Take the notes you'll need to compose brief letters, memos, and reports. That done, make phone calls. Get a bag of quarters or your long-distance calling card and spend the two-hour layover on all those calls you need to return or those you need to generate simply for goodwill or networking purposes.

The most difficult paperwork while traveling is composing long documents—reports, manuals, or procedures for which you need other bulky data at hand. But even those tasks can be manageable on the road if you have dictating equipment or a laptop computer. At least you can break the difficult task into small chunks, such as an outline of ideas to be incorporated into the document once you get back to office files.

Finally, use the same paper-handling principles on the road that you use in the office or at home. Sort and file as you go. Take along file folders marked "receipts," "correspondence," "to be filed," "phone calls," "travel arrangements," and "invoicing information" to make the paperwork you accumulate along the way manageable on the road and easy to dispose of when you return.

81. Listen to/Read Instructions, and Do It Right the First Time

Sometime in your social circle you've probably been the butt of the following joke in a group setting: You're handed a long list of crazy things to do and the emcee explains that the objective of the exercise is to see who completes the list of items first. The list contains actions such as, "Stand up and yell at the top of your lungs three times." "Pull off your shoes and hop around the room until you find someone whose birthday is the same day as yours." "Take off your belt and drop it in the paper bag in the center of the circle."

So immediately people begin to work through the list. The trick is this: The first item on the list says, "Read all these instructions before beginning to do anything." And the last item on the list says, "Ignore all the items above, sign your name on the top of this piece of paper, and sit back and watch the others make fools of themselves."

Do you recall how stupid you felt when in your haste to finish the list and "win" you didn't do what item 1 said (read everything first)? Isn't that the same feeling you have when time-consuming paperwork has to be redone?

Force yourself to read or listen to instructions. Think, then do.

As the old saying goes, "If you don't have time to do it right the first time, how will you ever find time to do it over?"

82. Don't Make To-Do Lists for the Pleasure of Crossing Off Items

Occasionally, I hear of someone so organized and productive that the work aids and principles become an end in themselves. Just for the "high" some people get upon completing a productive day or week, they resort to making out a new to-do list simply for the pleasure of crossing out items already done but which did not appear on the original list. The marked-up list itself becomes a reminder of accomplishments.

So they spend an extra ten minutes near the end of each day, jotting down everything they did so they can mark off the items one by one and feel that rush of adrenaline and sense of accomplishment.

Come on, now.

83. Ignore Responses that Can Be Directed Elsewhere

Flattery will get you every time: "You're always so helpful. Would you mind checking something for me? I know you attended the XYZ meeting last year and heard Ms. Smith's briefing on the new inventory system. Would you review your notes to see if..." While it's nice to be so "helpful" and efficient, the flattery almost always costs you time and effort.

Now that's not to say that you want to be unnecessarily rude, uncooperative, or unhelpful. It is to say that you can present alternatives for people: Do they want the information from you—if you can only get to it "in a few weeks"? Or, would they prefer to call Ted, "who has the same information at his fingertips"? When your helpfulness is presented in that framework, the other person will usually opt for the quicker alternative.

On other occasions, you simply don't have to respond at all. If the request requires time-consuming paperwork, simply stall until the requester seeks the information elsewhere.

You frequently make those decisions about your own needs. For example, you have a question about a contribution to your individual retirement account. You call your stockbroker's office, but she's not in.

You leave a message. She doesn't return the call that day. The next morning, in a hurry for the answer, you decide to phone your accountant to ask the same question. Instant answer. You're happy—and think nothing less of the "unavailable" stockbroker.

Likewise, others may ask you to provide information because you're convenient. And if you weren't so cooperative or convenient, they'd go elsewhere for the same information. Speedy help for them, less paperwork for you.

84. Sort and File Immediately

Paperwork just doesn't dispose of itself—unless you need it desperately, at which time it has disappeared forever all by itself.

On every incoming piece of paper or phone message, force yourself to sort and decide immediately. Out of sight is out of mind. Out of mind is focused time.

Either section off your work surface, make entries to your computer's reminder calendar, or use baskets/ files labeled accordingly: (1) To Do, (2) To

File, (3) To Pay, (4) To Pass On, (5) To Read Later. Don't lay a piece of paper down without placing it in one of these stacks/files/baskets.

The To File basket can become someone else's chore or can wait for you to do when you're brain dead and still have hours in the workday.

The To Pay pile can just lie there safely until every two weeks when you write checks.

The To Pass On pile contains paperwork routinely belonging to someone else or tasks you can delegate.

The To Read Later pile won't distract you because it doesn't need attention until you travel or need something to read in the dentist's office or in a meeting that's going nowhere. In other words, the reading pile won't stress you if that's decidedly a "downtime" task for your discretionary use.

The To Do pile becomes the only one that should stare back at you. You're focused and ready to go to work on one item at a time. Place these pieces of paper or reminder slips in priority order and focus on one paper project at a time until each is complete.

When your computer calendar reminds you to retrieve a paper and take action, jump on it.

If the paper won't go in one of these piles, computer files, or baskets, discard it and refuse to let it occupy any more of your time.

85. File Paperwork So that It's Retrievable

Records-retention experts tell us that 3 percent of the documents we file disappear into a big black hole. We never find them again. At the least, misfiled information frustrates and wastes our time.

Keep these tips in mind when filing:

- Choose a simple, alphabetical filing system that makes sense to anyone who happens to walk into your office.
- Avoid duplication of files. File it once and discard the other forty-six copies.
- File regularly. When the filing piles up, the individual assigned to this fun task grows weary quickly and just doesn't give a darn about where those last few pages go. File boxes that grow higher and higher strike fear in the hearts of others—fear to drop things into the box because they may need the document again before it ever gets into the files to be retrieved. Consequently, the paperwork that needs to be filed begins to pile up on individual desks, where it's "safe" and retrievable.
- Note at the top of the document where you want particular papers to go. For some items,

only you know why you're saving them and where and when you'll use the information again. Help your filing clerk help you in later retrieval by suggesting the appropriate file title or section.

- Put the most recent paper on top of the file because it will most likely be what you need first and most often. You don't want to have to sort through a stack each time you open the file.
- Purge your files regularly according to destroy dates (see tip 87).
- Never let a file walk out of your office. If you must travel with a certain file, put the file's contents into a temporary file by the same name and then return the documents to the permanent file when you're back in the office.

For those hard-to-decide-what-to-do-with items, here are some additional tips:

Catalogs/Order Forms. Put catalogs in a particular basket or on a shelf. When you need a catalog, go to that designated place and pick up the latest edition. Toss out the outdated copies without opening them.

Cartoons, Anecdotes, Statistics, and So Forth. File cartoons, jokes, anecdotes, or old speech outlines specifically by subject. Otherwise, you'll never want to attack the collection to find what you need for a certain occasion. If you already know how you'll use a cartoon, for example, file it by the upcoming event. If you don't have a particular use in mind, create a file section called "Research" and give it some subheading at the outset. You may later narrow or broaden that subject, but do begin with *some* subject rather than an all-inclusive generic title.

Maps. Put maps together in a file marked "Maps," being sure to note on each one where that map will take you.

Memorabilia/Photos. Put memorabilia in photo albums or boxes, clearly labeled. All those photos, announcements, and testimonial letters about how great you were as president of your professional association can be reviewed as a collection—out of the files and in a special book or box.

Procedures/Training Manuals. Procedural and training manuals are evolving documents. They're never final. If they're not kept up-to-date, they become useless. Updates, revisions, additions, and deletions must be made as they are decided, received, or sent. Procedures, although they add to the paperwork, save their weight in hours many times over when questions arise.

Prospect Records. Sales prospect records pay the bills. Don't chance letting little slips of paper handed to you in a restaurant get lost; those leads deserve attention. Get a notebook in which you can file sales prospect information by company. Or, set up a manual or computer file immediately by the prospect's name. Use a standard format to keep the information usable; you may want headings such as company name, contact name, address, phone number, directions to place of business, referred by, date of last interaction, results, next action/follow-up. Make the record format uniform so that you don't omit key information when you're in a hurry to record or transfer information.

Junk Mail. If you don't have an immediate use for junk mail, toss it before it ever reaches the files.

Think before you file. If the item is not worth putting in the right place, it's probably not worth keeping—a very reasonable conclusion. Toss it.

86. Treat Personal/Home Files as Seriously as You Do Business Files

When it comes to matters of life and death, your personal files are more important than your office files. Which gets more attention in *your* life? If you find your priority has been misplaced, determine to keep your personal files and paperwork as easily retrievable as your business files.

Although there are innumerable ways to set up

files, I've included the following topics as a starter kit for you. Add or eliminate as your own situation dictates:

Automobiles—Registration and Repair Records
    Buick
    Pontiac
    Toyota
Bank Statements
    First City
    NCNB
Budget
Catalogs
Certificates/Licenses/Official Records
    Birth Certificates
    Diplomas
    Divorce Decree
    Marriage Certificates
    Military
    Passports
    Social Security
    Transcripts
    Wills
Charities
    Church
    Goodwill
    Rosette Home
Clubs
    Dallas Credit Women's Association

    Kiwanis
    Parent Teacher Organization
    UT Alumni
Correspondence
    Family
    Outside
Credit Cards—Receipts/Payment Records
    American Express
    Chevron
    Dillard's
    Exxon
    Foley's
    MasterCard
    Visa
Entertainment
    Decorating Ideas
    Guest Lists
    Invitations/Printing
Contracts
    Maid Service
    Stevenson
Family Histories
Financial Summaries
    Computer Printouts—Monthly
    Net Worth Statements
Greeting Cards
    Jennifer
    Jim
    Joan
    Kevin

Susan
House
    Improvements
    Inventory
    Mortgage Payments
    Repairs
Insurance—Policies/Payment Records
    Boat
    Cars
    Health
    House
    Life
Investments
    Dreyfus Fund
    Dreyfus Liquid Assets
    Farm—San Antonio
    General Information/Advice
    IRA—Jim
    IRA—Joan
    Merrill Lynch CMA
    Merrill Lynch—Phoenix
    Rental—3557 Barclay Avenue
Medical
    Forms for Filing (Blanks)
    Health Records
    Receipts—Unfiled
    Receipts—Pending
    Receipts—Filed and Reimbursed
Miscellaneous
Pet Records

Dog
Horses
Résumés
Jim
Joan
Safety Deposit Box Contents (List)
School Records
Jennifer
Kevin
Susan
Subscriptions (Renewals)
Journals
Magazines
Newspapers
Taxes
Advice—Accountant/Lawyer
Current Year Receipts for Tax Purposes
General Information/Forms
Returns Filed and Receipts (By Year)
Travel (By Locale)
Maps
Utilities
Electricity
Gas
Telephone
Water/Garbage
Warranties/Instructions
Garden/Outside
Kitchen Appliances
Office Equipment
Miscellaneous

87. Put Destruction Dates on Paper

Several years ago while I was doing research for a book of model letters, I asked clients for samples from their own files. One records-retention manager just happened to be destroying four file drawers of correspondence from the office of a former CEO, who'd retired from the company ten years earlier. He offered me the files for my book. Thinking I'd found a real bonanza, I dug into the files with fervor. I could imagine what important documents were hidden there. A historical account of the big merger? A letter from the prime minister of England? A briefing on the celebrated patent infringement suit? Hardly.

What I found were these: an invitation to lunch with an old friend. A congratulatory letter from a colleague on the company's annual report. A letter thanking his hostess for a lovely weekend. A referral letter written on behalf of his chauffeur. Not exactly items that would interest company historians—or anybody for that matter. And the company had been paying to store those files for ten years!

(Storage of computer backups is no less time-consuming and also costly.)

An extreme case? No. Unfortunately, my research shows that to be the case all too often. We tend to clutter our files with things that have long outlived their usefulness—by anybody's standards.

How does that happen? One piece of paper at a time.

To avoid that clutter in your own files—clutter that you must continually sort through to find what you really want or need—always add a destruction date to anything that goes in the file temporarily. And much should be considered "temporary." Why should you keep a mail-out of the agenda of a meeting long after the meeting date? Why should you routinely keep a bid from Company A on equipment you've already purchased from Company B?

Instead, make it a habit on anything going into the files temporarily that you add a destroy notation, such as "D-2/16/93" (destroy after February 16, 1993), at the top of every paper.

88. Purge Your Files Every Time You Open Them

You've just read the previous tip on putting destroy dates on each piece of "temporary" paper. That habit simplifies this next step: Purge your files as you go. Anyone going through the files should immediately yank items that have a historical destroy date. The purge-as-you-go plan eliminates the need for a time-consuming massive purge at year's end.

Why be so concerned about that one little extra page in the files? Because that one little extra page soon becomes two, then three, then ten. And those ten extra pages keep you from quickly finding the one page you're looking for.

Likewise, don't be lulled into thinking that bulging files cause problems only at the office.

How about that kitchen drawer of cents-off product coupons? And that basketful of discount certificates for ordering pizza? And those notices from school about parents' night—three years ago? Whenever you see paper, check the date. If you've passed the drop-dead date for action or decision, discard the paper.

89. Cross-Reference Papers Rather than Make/Store Extra Copies

If you're collecting ideas for an upcoming chamber of commerce speech or a customer proposal and run across a ten-page trade journal article with just the appropriate statistics for both projects as well as two others, don't waste time by making four copies and filing the article in four different places. Duplicate copies clutter the files for later use.

Instead, simply clip the article and file it for the use that comes immediately to mind. Then drop a scrap of paper or index card into the other files with a brief notation such as this: "For statistics on customer-retention rates for service businesses, see XYZ article in Brown-Williamson file."

The cross-reference technique takes less time and space. And more importantly, it eliminates the danger of tossing out your only copy with the thought, "Oh, I have that filed several other places." Make duplicates only when you *remove* something from the files.

90. Put Paperwork Aside Only if You've Made a Complete Notation About What Needs to Be Done

You defeat the purpose of the principle "Handle each piece of paper only once" if you don't make adequate tickler notes before you get rid of the paper.

For example, you receive an invitation to serve on a panel on Tuesday evening of an upcoming convention. You can't respond immediately because you don't know if you'll be able to stay at the convention through Tuesday evening. That decision rests on the date of another client meeting in the city. A typical reaction is to jot a cryptic note on your calendar for a week later, "Call Steve about serving on the panel."

Then next week you read the note. "Oh, yeah. The panel. Why was I waiting on that? What time was the panel? What's Steve's phone number? His last name?" The cryptic note reminds you of the situation, but it's not detailed enough for you to take the required action without more paperwork shuffling—if you even remember where you put the original invitation with all the details.

Instead, an adequate tickler note would read: "After confirming my appointment with client Judson, call Steve Harris (123-5773) to tell him whether I'll serve on the convention panel on Tuesday evening at 7:00."

Set up a computer file or manual tickler file by date for the complete paperwork. Then on the appropriate date, all you need to do is check that file for reminders. Better yet, let the computer tap you on the shoulder.

All details are at hand. No extra paper shuffling. No lost time.

91. File Research by Use or Event, Not by Subject (Generally)

Think retrieval.

If you routinely clip statistics, articles, jokes and anecdotes, or whatever, most of the time a particular use, event, or issue has prompted your decision to clip and save. Unless you're a writer or speaker who keeps innumerable files of research for many uses, don't be tempted to file information by subject. Specifically, don't file by a subject so broad as "cartoons" or "sales statistics." You'll never find what you want later, or at best, you'll spend eons sorting through a bulging file to retrieve the right article.

Most people never again lay eyes on the information they've filed because retrieval seems too time-consuming and impossible.

Instead, file information by event or the use that prompted you to save the information in the first place. For example, if you think you might use certain statistics in a client proposal, file them in that client's file rather than by the subject of those statistics. If you intend to use the information in an upcoming seminar speech, file it "Speech—ASTD convention, May 19—."

An exception: If, like writers or speakers, you collect general information on many topics, break down your files as specifically as possible in your *research* section by subject: "HRD: Insurance." "HRD: 401K plans." "HRD: Salary Surveys."

Many people spend far too much time on retrieving information that they know is "in there somewhere." Before you decide to file, remember that *retrievable* info is the only *usable* info.

92. Request and Keep Multiple Copies of Official Documents

What a hassle to discover that before you can get your lost Social Security card replaced, you have to submit another copy of your birth certificate, marriage license, or whatever. That means a chain of paperwork.

You write the county where you were born to request the birth certificate and enclose the three-dollar fee. They send a form letter back saying the fee is now five dollars. You write a second letter, enclosing the correct fee and voiding the incorrect check in your check register. Then you write a second letter to the Social Security Administration, enclosing the requested birth certificate.

Then the mortgage company writes about your request to pay off the balance of the second lien on your house. They need your divorce decree papers. You write the lawyer who handled the divorce for the paperwork, which you must then forward to the mortgage company with a second letter.

Sound familiar?

Break the chain. Order and keep extra, official copies of the following documents for all members of your family:

- birth certificates
- marriage licenses
- divorce decrees
- death certificates
- wills
- health records
- college transcripts

If you have to order one from somewhere, order four. The extra fees will be much less expensive than your time in writing again and again for the official records. You'll love yourself later.

93. File Warranties and Instructions Logically and Permanently, with Receipts

"The icemaker on the refrigerator has stopped working, and I know it must still be under warranty."

"When did you purchase it, ma'am?"

"Just a few months ago."

"Okay, can you read me the model number—you'll find that either on the receipt or in the shaded box on the back page of the instruction booklet."

"Well, I can't find the receipt or booklet. But I know I bought it sometime last August because..."

Sound familiar? Avoid hassles with repairs, replacements, and refunds by filing your warranties, instruction booklets, and receipts together in one place.

Whether at the office or at home, staple your receipt and your warranty to the instruction booklet and file them all together in a big envelope. If you have numerous such purchases, you may decide to break them down further: "Warranties—kitchen appliances"; "Warranties—telephone equipment"; "Warranties—computer equipment."

Just remember that a warranty without a receipt or instructions (or vice versa) does little good. Spend a few seconds up front to eliminate the back-end headaches and paperwork shuffle.

94. Give Recognition to Achievements Not Recorded on Paper

Some managers give the impression that they judge activity by the mounds of paper subordinates send to their desk. Don't let your subordinates feel that the only thing that generates praise from you is paper. If they see that only written reports and summaries of their accomplishments get recognized, they'll continue to heap piles of paper on your desk "for your review."

When was the last time you verbally complimented someone for handling an angry customer on the phone? When was the last time you complimented a salesperson for taking an extra thirty minutes to build goodwill with a customer—goodwill that didn't show up on the current period's sales revenues? When was the last time you observed a team meeting and praised an employee for facilitating the meeting and leading members to an excellent problem resolution?

Save both you and your staff some paperwork time by giving oral recognition and praise on what you observe, what you hear from customers and colleagues, and what you feel and know firsthand—regardless of whether "the details" come in paper form to your desk.

Casual conversations, performance appraisals, staff meetings—all are appropriate occasions to give oral recognition.

95. Reward Ideas to Cut Paperwork

When your subordinates or colleagues send you something that you don't have a need for, ask why it was sent. Make it a big deal. Phone them or call them into your office for a discussion. Ask if they were writing simply to inform, to get approval, to get attention for the accomplishment, to get further direction, or to get a reaction. At the very least, your discussion and questioning will make them think twice before sending you meaningless paper in the future.

And when people come up with suggestions for eliminating unnecessary paperwork such as reports or unnecessary procedural steps, celebrate. Reward them with:

- money
- free tickets to an event
- lunch or dinner
- time off
- a mention in the company newsletter
- praise in a staff meeting

With recognition, you'll focus everyone's attention on eliminating unnecessary paperwork and procedures.

96. Don't Behead the Bearer of Bad News

Some staffers write voluminous memos and reports because they fear delivering bad news face-to-face. Check your own response to bad news when someone telephones or walks into your office with a tale of woe. If you explode, you'll get fewer and fewer telephone calls or visits and more and more paper to read.

And not only will you get more to read, but you'll often get paperwork that's more *difficult* to read. When people fear to be direct with negative responses, the bad news may be so buried and understated that you'll have to read the document several times to find out the real intent. And you must then schedule a meeting or a follow-up telephone call to reevaluate what was supposedly communicated in the written document.

A far more serious result is that the buried news comes too late for you to take corrective action.

Accept bad news graciously, and you'll get it more directly and in time to minimize its effects.

97. Let Others Know They Can Be Straightforward with You

How do you let others know they can be straightforward with you? By setting the example yourself. If subordinates and colleagues observe your attempts to hide bad news from clients or bosses, they'll do the same in communicating—or not communicating—with you.

When the silence is deafening on a particular project, nudge the employee with questions such as: "I haven't heard much from you on the Bidden project. I'm guessing that you may have run into some difficulties there. Let's discuss where you are on that."

Or: "The project I assigned you last month was full of pitfalls. Tell me how you're working your way through the mine field. What's going as you expected and what do we have problems with?"

Such wording lets subordinates know you expect reality and truth. Consequently, they'll tend to give you information in time for you to correct a faulty course of action. And, likewise, their written communication will usually be open and straightforward when they know your focus will be on corrective action and guidance rather than on blame.

Honest communication always means less paperwork.

98. Use a Clipping Service for Subjects of Interest

Rather than subscribe to dozens of journals, magazines, and newspapers, hire a clipping service to gather information for you. Do you want them to clip ads and articles on your competition? On the subject of nuclear energy? On training budgets of Fortune 500 companies? Cartoons on political figures? Whatever your interest, consider letting someone else's eyes do the reading and fingers do the clipping.

The following national clipping services provide a variety of time-saving services for their subscribers. Call or write them for more information.

Bacon's Information, Inc.
332 South Michigan Avenue
Chicago, IL 60604
1-800-621-0561

Burrelle's Information Services
75 E. Northfield Road
Livingston, NJ 07039
1-800-631-1160

Luce Press Clippings
420 Lexington Avenue
New York, NY 10170
1-800-528-8226

99. Don't Let Your Computer Reproduce Endlessly and Aimlessly

Whatever happened to the idea that computers would create and revolutionize the workplace? You and I both know that the computer really compounds the paperwork problem by making it so easy

- to edit (helping us to write, read, and revise fourteen drafts of a report)
- to send electronic mail to the world (adding to everyone's reading)
- to get a printout of data compiled in eighty-six different formats (confusing interpretation of the facts)
- to print out multiple copies (cluttering up everybody's files)

Alas, people are still necessary to make judgment calls about the proliferation of paper.

Although at times you've probably operated computers that seemed to have a mind of their own, exercise your own judgment about the point of diminishing returns. Is the report so formal and the results so significant that you need to edit and revise it for the twenty-fourth time? Does everyone in Accounting really need the printout in such detail? Does Harry in Shipping really need a copy of the full report on October sales projections?

Awareness and judgment mark the intelligent computer user.

100. Cancel Free Subscriptions that You Wouldn't Buy

Americans love getting things for free. If you don't believe it, see how many people stop to accept a free sample of crackers from the smiling rep in the grocery store. See how many "giveaway" pencils, jar openers, key chains, and calendars you have lying around your house or office.

So when free magazines, journals, or memberships arrive in our mailboxes, we often accept them as if they were vital to our mental or physical health or to our business or client relationships.

Somewhere on the masthead inside the first few pages, we see clearly printed that this subscription "costs" seventy-nine dollars a year. A seventy-nine-dollar value—ours absolutely free. Now smart people wouldn't toss seventy-nine dollars away without investigating, would they? So, we add these pieces of paper to our reading pile as if they had somehow been assigned to us to complete as part of our job.

Take a closer look at these freebies. Are there just one or two informative tidbits on the opening pages to tempt us to open the magazine or newsletter, while the rest reminds us to buy the organization's products or services? No harm in reading the one or two useful tidbits—*if* we stop there. But many of us feel compelled to continue through the other articles and ads.

Guard your reading time. If you wouldn't pay someone *money* for the privilege of reading the newsletter, magazine, journal, or brochure, should you pay with your *time*?

101. Discard Unread Magazines, Journals, and Newspapers

Piles of journals, newspapers, and magazines discourage even the most avid reader. Researchers/psychologists refer to this mental state as "information overload syndrome."

Although you watch the stack growing, you hesitate to discard the issues because *you paid for them,* right? To toss them out would be like tossing away money.

But what have you gained by letting them stack up in the corner? To rid yourself of the stress and the paper, you have three alternatives:

- Have an assistant go through them and clip articles that are on subjects of interest to you.
- Have an assistant copy the contents page in each and let you check the ones you want clipped and filed for a *specific* use.
- Discard every issue that's more than three months old—no questions asked, no pages opened.

If the pileup situation repeats itself, then cancel your subscriptions to one-fourth of the magazines, journals, or newspapers there. If that doesn't correct the problem, repeat the process.

FOR MORE INFORMATION

Dianna Booher travels internationally to speak and present seminars and workshops on the following topics:

Get the Paperwork Off Your Desk

Write This Way to Success

Communication: The Quality and Productivity Links

Communication: From Boardroom to Bedroom

Communicating CARE to Customers

Support Staff as Team Members

Did You Hear What I Think I Said?

How Will You Know When You Arrive?

You Are Your Future

If you would like more information about having Dianna speak to your group, write or phone our Dallas-Fort Worth office:

Booher Consultants, Inc.
1010 W. Euless Blvd. Suite 150
Euless, TX   76039-2150
1-800-342-6621